English
Olympiad

Class 07

A must have book for all
Olympiads & Talent Search Exams...

by
Amit Tanwar

BLOOM CAP
Bloom Cap Edu Ventures Pvt. Ltd.

Bloom Cap Edu Ventures Pvt. Ltd.

Administrative & Production Office

'Ramchhaya' 4577/15, Agarwal Road, Darya Ganj, New Delhi -110002
Tele: 011- 47630600, 43518550

ISBN: 978-93-25519-26-8

PRICE: ₹100.00

PO No: TXT-XX-XXXXXXX-X-XX

For further information about the books log on to
www.bloomcap.org

Follow us on

Preface

"Future belongs to those Who prepares for it today"

School Olympiads are National & International level competitions conducted by different Government, Non-Government & Educational Organisations with the purpose of making the children ready to face competitive exams.

The challenging Questions asked in Olympiads motivate them to learn more & more and bring out the best results with improved academic performance. The Awards & Scholarship offered by Olympiads motivate children to aspire & strive for doing better and emerge out to be the best.

English Olympiads

English is one of the most widely spoken languages across the world. In today's era, good command over English is considered as a must have skill. The greatest advantage of studying English is improvement in communication skills along with the growth of personality.

English Olympiads are meant to strengthen students' command over this universal language by improving spellings, grammar, sentence structure and to master student's language skills.

'Bloom English Olympiad Study Book Class 7' is a perfect resource to Study & Practice for Olympiad Exams and other National & State Level Talent Search Exams & Other Competitions.

Some Special Features of Bloom English Olympiad Study Books are;

- Complete coverage of all the aspects of English; Grammar, Reading Comprehension, Writing Skills, Spellings, Vocabulary & Communication Skills.
- Chapterwise Exercises having different types of Objective Questions at par with the Olympiad Level.
- Olympiad Pattern Practice Sets at the end.

This book is prepared by Expert Panel with the utmost care, still if you have any suggestions regarding its improvement then feel free to contact us at olympiads@bloomcap.org. We will try to inculcate your suggestions in the further editions.

Contents

Noun

1 Mark Questions

Directions (Q. Nos. 1-7) Read the statements given below and identify the noun from the given sentences.

1. We bought three pieces of furniture yesterday from the mega sale.
   (a) bought   (b) furniture
   (c) from   (d) mega

2. I have a dream of going into space, have you ever boarded a spaceship?
   (a) Spaceship   (b) you
   (c) ever   (d) boarded

3. Courage is an admirable quality. It is not found in everyone.
   (a) found   (b) admirable
   (c) everyone   (d) courage

4. I am so proud that both my sons serve the nation. They are in the army.
   (a) proud   (b) army
   (c) serve   (d) Both (a) and (b)

5. I always wanted to be a photographer and my family stood by me.
   (a) family   (b) always
   (c) stood   (d) Both (a) and (c)

6. What our country needs today is peace and good governance.
   (a) What   (b) needs
   (c) our   (d) None of these

7. My membership card for the Cricket club expires tomorrow.
   (a) club   (b) expires
   (c) my   (d) for

Directions (Q. Nos. 8-12) Pick out all the noun in the sentences given below.

8. The boys and girls played in the school ground.
   (a) boys, played, school, ground
   (b) boys, girls, ground, school
   (c) girls, the, and, played, school
   (d) boys, girls, the, school, ground

9. We went to the theatre to watch a movie.
   (a) we, theatre, watch, movie
   (b) watch, movie
   (c) theatre, movie
   (d) we, theatre, movie

10. Sudha is a very popular Kathak dancer.
    (a) Sudha, popular, Kathak, dancer
    (b) Sudha, very, dancer
    (c) Sudha, popular, dancer
    (d) Sudha, dancer, kathak

11. He cooked the dinner tonight in a microwave.
    (a) he, cooked, microwave
    (b) dinner, microwave
    (c) tonight, microwave
    (d) cooked, dinner, microwave

12. This building is entirely made up of glass.
  (a) building, glass
  (b) this, building, entirely, glass
  (c) this, made, up, glass
  (d) building, entirely, glass

Directions (Q. Nos. 13-17) Fill in the blanks with the correct form of nouns.

13. I want some .... about the syllabus of BA LLB course.
  (a) informations
  (b) information
  (c) Both (a) and (b)
  (d) None of the above

14. The boy was the .... of a poor single mother.
  (a) son   (b) sons
  (c) son's   (d) Both (a) and (b)

15. Vibha and Vibha's mother are ....
  (a) doctors   (b) doctor's
  (c) doctor   (d) Both (a) and (c)

16. Keep the .... at a safe place.
  (a) gun
  (b) guns
  (c) Both (a) and (b)
  (d) None of the above

17. A few .... are standing on the stairs of that temple.
  (a) woman   (b) women
  (c) man   (d) Both (a) and (b)

Directions (Q. Nos. 18-22) Fill in the blanks with suitable nouns.

18. This musical .... is the finest in this ....
  (a) troupe, world
  (b) bunch, Delhi
  (c) group, America
  (d) band, city

19. I don't have much ...., just one small ....
  (a) luggages, bag   (b) bags, luggage
  (c) luggage, bag   (d) luggage, bags

20. We went on a jungle safari and were lucky to spot a .... of ....
  (a) group, lion   (b) pride, lions
  (c) flock, bird   (d) Both (b) and (c)

21. .... fly in the ....
  (a) Bird, sky   (b) Birds, skies
  (c) Bird, skies   (d) Birds, sky

22. He fell down a .... of stairs and hurt his ....
  (a) flight, knee   (b) flight, knees
  (c) cast, knees   (d) Both (a) and (b)

Directions (Q. Nos. 23-28) Identify the type of noun (underlined) used in the following sentences.

23. The State Government appointed a <u>committee</u> of six to assess the situation.
  (a) Proper noun
  (b) Collective noun
  (c) Uncountable noun
  (d) Abstract noun

24. Yamuna, like the Ganga, is a holy <u>river</u> of India.
  (a) Common noun   (b) Countable noun
  (c) Concrete noun   (d) All of these

25. The employee was awarded for his <u>sincerity</u> by the management.
  (a) Abstract noun   (b) Proper noun
  (c) Concrete noun   (d) Common noun

26. The medals are made up of <u>gold, silver and bronze</u>.
  (a) All collective noun
  (b) All common noun
  (c) All uncountable noun
  (d) All abstract noun

27. The <u>conference</u> was attended by all the students as there is 100 per cent attendance.
(a) Collective noun   (b) Proper noun
(c) Common noun   (d) Abstract noun

28. Steam engine was invented by <u>James Watt</u>.
(a) Countable noun   (b) Abstract noun
(c) Proper noun   (d) Collective noun

2 Marks Questions

Directions (Q. Nos. 29 and 30) Read the sentences carefully and choose the option with correct usage of noun.

29. A. I gave him a few advice.
B. A herd of cattle was grazing nearby.
C. We faced trouble in driving through the mountains.
D. Please pass a glass of water to me.
Codes
(a) Only option B is correct
(b) Both B and D are correct
(c) B, C and D are correct
(d) Only D is correct

30. A. There are no cuckoos in the woods.
B. I have two handkerchief.
C. Buy me three kilo potato.
D. Do you have any proves against him?
Codes
(a) Only A is correct
(b) A, B and D are correct
(c) C and D are correct
(d) None of the above

31. Each has a house, yes, even a mouse.
But there's never a home, better than my own.
How many common nouns are there in this short poem?
(a) 3   (b) 4
(c) 2   (d) 5

32. Last Sunday, Jim and John went to fly kites. Jim's kite looked like a butterfly while John's kite looked like a star.
Which noun is not present in this sentence?
(a) Concrete noun
(b) Abstract noun
(c) Common noun
(d) All nouns are present

33. Match the following.

	List I		List II
A.	Abstract noun	1.	Forests
B.	Concrete noun	2.	Electricity
C.	Uncountable noun	3.	Wickedness
D.	Common noun	4.	State

Codes

	A	B	C	D		A	B	C	D
(a)	2	4	1	3	(b)	3	1	2	4
(c)	1	3	4	2	(d)	2	4	3	1

34. Match the following nouns with their correct use.

	List I		List II
A.	A bunch of	1.	Gypsies
B.	A range of	2.	Keys
C.	A caravan of	3.	Singers
D.	A choir of	4.	Mountains

Codes

	A	B	C	D
(a)	3	4	2	1
(b)	2	3	4	1
(c)	1	2	4	3
(d)	2	4	1	3

Pronoun

1 Mark Questions

Directions (Q. Nos. 1-7) Read the statements given below and identify the pronoun from the given sentences.

1. Can you hand me that hammer as I need to nail in the wall?
(a) can   (b) that
(c) hammer   (d) in

2. I will not tell anything about this incident to anyone. Please be assured.
(a) anyone   (b) not
(c) tell   (d) incident

3. Sanchi is the name of my 2 year old daughter and she is the favourite of everyone.
(a) everyone   (b) name
(c) the   (d) old

4. Each participant will be given equal chance of winning, so just put in your best effort.
(a) chance   (b) equal
(c) each   (d) participant

5. Do you know that somebody is coming to our house for dinner tonight.
(a) somebody
(b) tonight
(c) our
(d) Both (a) and (c)

6. I am unable to go myself so request you to drop me at the metro station today.
(a) myself   (b) station
(c) at   (d) the

7. Meet this person as this is the person whom I love dearly.
(a) this
(b) whom
(c) I
(d) All of the above

Directions (Q. Nos. 8-14) Fill in the blanks with the most suitable pronoun from the given options.

8. You are having such a headache; did you get .... a cup of tea?
(a) himself   (b) herself
(c) yourself   (d) itself

9. My parents live in the beautiful hill station of Munnar. .... often go to see them.
(a) we   (b) us
(c) they   (c) them

10. .... show will be hosted by Ritu.
(a) This
(b) That
(c) These
(d) Both (a) and (b)

11. .... of us got a diamond necklace as inheritance.
   (a) Anyone   (b) Each
   (c) Everyone   (d) All of these

12. The king and queen were fair and just during .... reign.
   (a) their   (b) theirs   (c) their's   (d) they

13. Mom drove .... to school today.
   (a) him   (b) her
   (c) me   (d) All of these

14. .... who live in glass houses, should not throw stone at others.
   (a) One   (b) Those
   (c) These   (d) Everyone

Directions (Q. Nos. 15-21) Fill in the blanks with the most suitable pronouns from the given options.

15. Let .... know .... much milk is to be added into the cake mixture.
   (a) us, which
   (b) me, how
   (c) them, which
   (d) Both (b) and (c)

16. .... are tall trees on .... side of the road that makes for a beautiful walk.

   (a) There, either   (b) Their, each
   (c) Those, either   (d) These, each

17. He .... posted the letter yesterday and now he has forgotten all about ....
   (a) has, it   (b) himself, that
   (c) had, him   (d) himself, it

18. .... who got to the canteen late had trouble finding .... seat.
   (a) No one, ours
   (b) Anyone, her
   (c) Everyone, their
   (d) Everyone, theirs

19. .... has two sons and three daughters and all the children love .... a lot.
   (a) I, one another   (b) He, one another
   (c) She, one another (d) Both (b) and (c)

20. I know ....victory is possible only when .... play as a team.
   (a) our, we   (b) their , they
   (c) that, we   (d) All of these

21. The answer was .... true nor false, ... was a tricky question.
   (a) neither, it   (b) either, that
   (c) neither, that   (d) Both (a) and (c)

Directions (Q. Nos. 22-26) Replace the underlined nouns with suitable pronouns to make an appropriate paragraph.

The fortune teller moved her dry hands over the glass ball that **22.** <u>fortune teller</u> had bought a long time ago. She could hear the laughter and shouts of children as **23.** <u>children</u> ran from one tent to the other. The teenagers were eager to hear about the horrific stories, mysterious strangers living in far off lands. So the fortune teller told **24.** <u>teenagers</u> what they wanted to hear. Just then a young man with a timid smile appeared. The fortune teller took his trembling hands into **25.** <u>hands</u> and peered at the revealing lines of **26.** <u>young man's</u> palm.

22. (a) he   (b) she
     (c) herself   (d) no change

23. (a) their   (b) we
     (c) us   (d) they

24. (a) them   (b) her
     (c) everybody   (d) no change

25. (a) her's   (b) hers   (c) her   (d) ours

26. (a) its   (b) his   (c) her   (d) their

2 Marks Questions

27. Complete this sentence with the pronoun that agrees with the words in underline.

Zumba dancer <u>Bridget</u> may have started .... career in a small town of North Carolina, but it was the tour of Canada that made .... a big star.

(a) herself, her   (b) her, it
(c) her, her   (d) hers, her

28. Fill in the blanks with a pronoun used in place of the proper noun in underline.

<u>Damodar</u> became very wealthy as a Table player, after .... long career; .... left most of his money to a charitable hospital in his home town.

(a) a, its
(b) having, him
(c) his, he
(d) that, he

29. Read the sentences and choose the correct option.

A. I went to the house of mine cousin.
B. Each person has a chance.
C. These questions may be easy.
D. Myself study in class VII.
Codes
(a) Only A   (b) Both B and C
(b) Only D   (d) All of these

30. Which among the following sentence is error free?

A. Several have suggested canceling the meeting.
B. This dog is their's.
C. You were winners this year.
D. She was coming to meet us tonight.
Codes
(a) Only A
(b) Only C

(c) Both A and D
(d) None of the above

31. Match the following.

	List I		List II
A.	Possessive pronoun	1.	Someone
B.	Demonstrative pronoun	2.	Ourselves
C.	Reflexive pronoun	3.	Those
D.	Indefinite pronoun	4.	Mine

Codes

	A	B	C	D
(a)	3	1	4	2
(b)	4	3	2	1
(c)	1	3	4	2
(d)	2	4	1	3

32. Match the following.

	List I		List II
A.	Personal pronoun	1.	Whom were you speaking to at the party yesterday?
B.	Emphatic pronoun	2.	Only you are allowed to attend the party.
C.	Relative pronoun	3.	The book itself tells you all about pronouns.
D.	Interrogative pronoun	4.	This is the boy who scored the highest marks.

Codes

	A	B	C	D			A	B	C	D
(a)	3	2	4	1		(b)	2	1	3	4
(c)	2	3	4	1		(d)	4	3	1	2

Chapter 03

Verbs

1 Mark Questions

Directions (Q. Nos. 1-7) Identify the verb in these sentences.

1. He took a great risk in applying for a job in the same company where he worked two years before.
   (a) risk
   (b) took
   (c) same company
   (d) two years before

2. I never want to see that horrible look on his face again. I just can't bear it.
   (a) see
   (b) face
   (c) that horrible
   (d) I never

3. Lot of Italian families were living in my neighbourhood at that time.
   (a) lot of
   (b) neighbourhood
   (c) in my first
   (d) were living

4. Captain Arunesh was a true patriot who would die for his country.
   (a) true patriot
   (b) would die
   (c) country
   (d) for his

5. Don't call them at this hour. They may be having dinner.
   (a) at this hour
   (b) may be having
   (c) don't call
   (d) Both (b) and (c)

6. Everyone was surprised when Tarun lost his phone shortly after he had bought it.
   (a) surprised
   (b) had bought
   (c) bought
   (d) All of these

7. Nikita started doing her homework only after she finished her novel.
   (a) only after
   (b) started doing
   (c) she finished her
   (d) Both (b) and (c)

Directions (Q. Nos. 8-12) Read the sentences and match the subject with a suitable verb by choosing the correct option.

8. Hari ran with quick steps to his house when it .... raining all of a sudden.
   (a) start
   (b) starting
   (c) started
   (d) None of these

9. A good citizen .... all his financial obligations on time.
   (a) perform
   (b) performs
   (c) is performing
   (d) performing

10. During the test, the classroom was so quiet that you .... even a pin drop.
    (a) will hear
    (b) may be hearing
    (c) hear
    (d) could hear

11. People realised much later that the Earth .... around the Sun.
    (a) goes
    (b) go
    (c) Both (a) and (b)
    (d) None of these

12. The terrified people of that tribe .... to the mountains for safety.
    (a) flee
    (b) fleeing
    (c) have fled
    (d) fled

Directions (Q. Nos. 13-15) Fill in the blanks with the most suitable verbs or form of verbs.

13. .... over the sea was a bit scary, the first time I .... an airplane.
    (a) To fly, rode
    (b) Flying, rode
    (c) Fly, ride
    (d) Flying, was riding

14. I .... the .... of the movie as I .... late at the theatre.
    (a) missed, beginning, arrived
    (b) miss, beginning, was arrived
    (c) will miss, beginning, will be arriving
    (d) is missing , beginning, is arriving

15. My brother and I .... our uncle last night to .... him Happy Birthday.
    (a) phone, wished
    (b) phoned, wished
    (c) phone, wish
    (d) phoned, wish

Directions (Q. Nos. 16-21) Read the following paragraph carefully and see if the underlined verbs are in their correct form. If not replace them with the options.

I ....(16).... . 1 <u>wake</u> up one lazy morning and discovered that my slippers ....(17).... <u>are missed</u>. I remember it very clearly that I ....(18).... <u>placed</u> them on the small door mat just outside my room the last night. I ....(19).... <u>searched</u> high and low for them in the entire house, when all of a sudden my younger brother rushed in. He came into my room, and ....(20).... <u>had exclaimed</u> loudly "Come quickly! The neighbour's dog Alan has taken away all our shoes. No doubt I ....(21).... <u>astonish</u> on thinking about Alan, coming to our house during night time or at the wee hours of the morning and taking away all our shoes. Upon seeing that dog, we gave him a chase. But the dog was too fast for us. Our neighbours also looked for our shoes inside their house. Unfortunately, we could not retrieve our shoes and to this day, nobody knows what happened to our shoes.

16. (a) waking   (b) woke
    (c) awake   (d) No change

17. (a) were missing
    (b) are missing
    (c) will be missing
    (d) No change

18. (a) have placed   (b) had placed
    (c) has placed   (d) No change

19. (a) am searching
    (b) was searching
    (c) will be searching
    (d) No change

20. (a) exclaim   (b) exclaiming
    (d) exclaimed   (d) No change

21. (a) am astonished
    (b) have been astonished
    (c) was astonished
    (d) No change

Directions (Q. Nos. 22-26) Read the following passage and fill in each blank with the correct form of verb.

Tea is a beverage ......(22)...... by many past generations of people.

Tea is one of the major and high earning plantation crop of India. Workers, working in tea plantations ......(23)...... up the tea leaves from the tea bushes. These bushes are kept at a height of about 1-2 meters only by regular pruning, in order to form the 'plucking table' which facilitates hand plucking and .....(24)....... bud growth. After the tea leaves are gathered, they are dried and roasted at varying temperatures to get the right kind of flavour and aroma. There are many different ways of preparing tea as it .....(25)....... in liquor form with milk or mixed with honey and lemon. .....**(26)**....... teas add aromas and flavours to the base tea. This can be accomplished by adding flavouring agents like Jasmine, ginger, mint etc.

22. (a) drink   (b) drank
    (c) drunk   (d) drinking

23. (a) picked   (b) pick
    (c) are picking   (d) have been picking

24. (a) encourage
    (b) will encourage
    (c) encouraged
    (d) encourages

25. (a) will be served
    (b) can be served
    (c) is serve
    (d) may be served

26. (a) Flavour and scent
    (b) Flavouring and scented
    (c) Flavoured and scented
    (d) Flavoured and scent

2 Marks Questions

27. Replace the underlined words with suitable words.
Everything <u>been done to prevent</u> the river from bursting its banks during the heavy flow of the upcoming monsoons.
A. been done in preventing
B. has been done to prevent
C. have been done to prevent
D. No error
Codes
(a) Only A   (b) Only B
(c) Both C and D   (d) Only C

28. Choose the option with the correct use of modal verbs. The modal verbs are in bold.
1. Winters in Shimla **can be** really cold
2. Winters in Shimla **could be** really cold.
3. Winters in Shimal **would be** really cold
4. Winters in Shimla **should be** really cold.
(a) 1   (b) 2   (c) 3   (d) 4

29. Consider the following sentences.
1. Unfortunately I didn't was in Jaipur.
2. If I had your address, I would have sent you a postcard.

Which of these statements is/are correct?
(a) Only 1
(b) Only 2
(c) Both 1 and 2
(d) None of these

30. Replace the word in italics with phrasal verbs.
The number of people in prison has been *increasing* steadily over the past ten years.
A. going off   B. going on
C. going up   D. going away
(a) Only A
(b) Only B
(c) Only C
(d) Both A and D

Adverbs

1 Mark Questions

Directions (Q. Nos. 1-5) Choose the adverbs in the following sentences.

1. They mostly go out in the evening as the day time is very cold here and afternoons are rather hot.
   (a) hot　　　　　(b) mostly
   (c) day time　　　(d) evening

2. My grandparents live in the city of Pune and I occasionally pay them a visit.
   (a) city of
   (b) a visit
   (c) occasionally
   (d) live in the

3. The little boy shyly went up to the cashier and admitted that he took the toy without paying.
   (a) shyly
   (b) paying
   (c) little
   (d) without

4. Sally works continuously and she never stops in between. She has a record of completing all the work on time.
   (a) never
   (b) continuously
   (c) work
   (d) Both (a) and (b)

5. I wanted to be friendly so I tried hard to think of something to say.
   (a) friendly　　　(b) hard
   (c) tried　　　　(d) Both (a) and (b)

Directions (Q. Nos. 6-15) Fill in the blanks with the correct adverb. Choose from the options given.

6. I .... want to know what happened.
   (a) exactly　　　(b) purely
   (c) simply　　　(d) highly

7. Don't worry. It's .... safe. You won't fall.
   (a) finely　　　(b) deeply
   (c) fully　　　　(d) largely

8. The future will be .... shaped by technology.
   (a) merely　　　(b) specially
   (c) largely　　　(d) purely

9. Everything will be .... cheaper in the sales.
   (a) widely　　　(b) greatly
   (c) considerably　(d) particularly

10. There's nothing .... similar to this product.
    (a) closely
    (b) remotely
    (c) nearly
    (d) wildly

11. I am sure that we'll succeed ....
(a) hardly   (b) entirely
(c) eventually   (d) deeply

12. Nobody answering the phone doesn't .... mean there is no one there.
(a) necessarily   (b) surely
(c) wholly   (d) strictly

13. It's .... true that education is becoming global.
(a) exactly   (b) reliably
(c) certainly   (d) fully

14. We were .... considering selling the house.
(a) heavily   (b) seriously
(c) brightly   (d) fully

15. It was a long time ago, but I .... do remember when we first arrived in our new home.
(a) specially   (b) surely
(c) seriously   (d) strictly

Directions (Q. Nos. 16-20) Fill in the blanks with correct adverbs by choosing from the given options.

16. The building is leaning .... We should .... evacuate it.
(a) dangerous, quick
(b) dangerous, quickly
(c) dangerously, quickly
(d) dangerously, quick

17. They can do the Maths problems .... They think Maths is an .... subject.
(a) conveniently, easy
(b) easily, easy
(c) tough, toughly
(d) easy, convenient

18. Nothing we needed for our study was .... at hand or .... obtained.
(a) close, easily   (b) nearby, at once
(c) available, easily (d) closely, easy

19. Rakesh was .... excited. His team had .... won the trophy.
(a) horribly, easiest
(b) extremely, easy
(c) horrible, easy
(d) extremely, easily

20. I did the homework .... by myself. I'm an .... student.
(a) completely, intelligent
(b) whole, studious
(c) all, perfect
(d) fully, full

Directions (Q. Nos. 21-24) Select suitable adverbs from the options given to complete the given paragraph.

The Indian soldiers at the Siachen glacier got up early in the morning. The night had been ....(21)....... cold. They had wrapped themselves carefully with as many woollen clothes as they could, but to no avail. A cold wind blew .....(22)...... in the valley. There had been an avalanche nearby. The soldiers were tense and worried. They silently ate their breakfast. .....(23)......., they moved towards their positions. The General was worried whether the enemy had secretly moved nearer. .....(24)......., the enemy had attacked more frequently.

21. (a) dreadfully   (b) believably
(c) snowingly   (d) temperately

22. (a) quietly   (b) slowly
(c) quickly   (d) violently

23. (a) Cheerfully
(b) Cheeringly
(c) Anxiously
(d) Sadly

24. (a) Previously   (b) Recently
(c) Suddenly   (d) Usually

2 Marks Questions

25. Choose the sentence/s that shows the correct use of adverb.

1. They go out in the week very seldom.
2. Do you go always to cinema on Fridays?
3. Her usually calm face showed excitement.

Codes

(a) 1 and 3   (b) 1 and 2
(c) 2 and 3   (d) Only 3

26 Put the adverbs given in brackets in the correct position in the sentence.
'The Fault is yours.' No, it isn't. You are at fault".(entirely, equally)

A. 'The Fault is yours entirely.' No, it isn't equally. You are at fault'.
B. 'The Fault is entirely yours.' No, it isn't. You are equally at fault'.
C. 'The Fault is yours.' No, entirely it isn't. You are equally at fault'.
D. 'The Fault entirely is yours.' No, it isn't. You equally are at fault'.

Codes

(a) Both A   (b) Only B
(c) Both C and D   (d) None of these

27. Choose the sentence with the correct order of the adverb.

1. My brother had enough sleep barely.
2. He sincerely asked me to move seats.
3. I joyously shouted at the top of my lungs.
4. I have been waiting patiently for two hours.

Codes

(a) Both 1 and 2   (b) 1, 2 and 3
(c) 2, 3 and 4   (d) All of these

28. Match the following to make meaningful sentences.

	List I		List II
A.	This room is strictly	1.	By himself.
B.	The guards were sleeping	2.	Share prices dropped sharply.
C.	He always goes jogging	3.	Meant for teachers only.
D.	When the war broke out	4.	Soundly when the thieves broke in.

Codes

	A	B	C	D			A	B	C	D
(a)	4	1	2	3		(b)	3	1	4	2
(c)	3	4	1	2		(d)	1	4	2	3

29. Match the following to put the correct adverb at the end of the sentences.

	List I		List II
A.	The boy is so rude, he shouted	1.	anywhere
B.	Sometimes we have to take a step	2.	well
C.	They are already there, but we are not going	3.	backwards
D.	She is a good dancer, she dances	4.	loudly

Codes

	A	B	C	D			A	B	C	D
(a)	3	4	2	1		(b)	4	3	1	2
(c)	2	1	4	3		(d)	1	2	4	3

Chapter 05

Adjectives

1 Mark Questions

Directions (Q. Nos. 1-6) Identify the adjectives in the sentences given below.

1. Next Sunday is a very special day for me. It's my mum and dad's anniversary.
   (a) next
   (b) anniversary
   (c) special
   (d) Both (a) and (c)

2. Have you seen the change? The days are getting warmer and bigger as we near summers.
   (a) seen, warmer
   (b) change, bigger
   (c) summers
   (d) warmer, bigger

3. I am quite fat now but I was much thinner when I was younger.
   (a) younger, fat
   (b) thinner, younger, fat
   (c) quite, much, thinner,
   (d) thinner, younger, fat, quite, much

4. Of course! I know that my daughter is the most beautiful girl in that group.
   (a) beautiful
   (b) most beautiful
   (c) group, beautiful
   (d) know, beautiful

5. Please be careful everyone. The floor is slippery as I mopped it just now.
   (a) mopped
   (b) careful
   (c) slippery
   (d) careful, slippery

6. May I have a clean plate? This one is very dirty.
   (a) clean, dirty
   (b) plate, clean, dirty
   (c) clean, very, dirty
   (d) clean

Directions (Q. Nos. 7-12) Fill in the blanks with suitable adjectives.

7. Ancient, ... coins are exhibited in this museum.
   (a) old
   (b) precious
   (b) cheap
   (d) lifeless

8. These cakes are burnt. I have to make a .... one for the evening when my guests will come.
   (a) old   (b) later   (c) new   (d) stale

9. There are ....apples on the plate.
   (a) some green
   (b) fewer red
   (c) least golden
   (d) most greener

10. The man who is performing today is a .... person.
    (a) most famous
    (b) well
    (c) well-known
    (d) more known

11. My dog has .... eyes and .... skin.
    (a) blue, fluffy
    (b) red, softest
    (c) green, swollen
    (d) white, softer

12. I have got a .... money, it is .... to buy this book.
    (a) little, few
    (b) fewer, not enough
    (c) few, little
    (d) little, enough

Direction (Q. Nos. 13-20) Fill in the blanks with the correct form of adjectives. Choose from the given options.

13. This is the .... painting he has ever made.
    - (a) more beautiful
    - (b) beautiful
    - (c) beautier
    - (d) most beautiful

14. My luggage is .... than yours.
    - (a) heavy
    - (b) heaviest
    - (c) heavier
    - (d) heavily

15. The rides at the fair were .... than I thought.
    - (a) expensive
    - (b) more expensive
    - (c) most expensive
    - (d) not expensive

16. Ravi is more .... than expected.
    - (a) lately (b) late (c) later (d) latter

17. I saw a rainbow in the sky. It was the .... sight that I had ever seen.
    - (a) splendid
    - (b) splendier
    - (c) most splendid
    - (d) more splendid

18. They claim that the new computers are ....
    - (a) most sturdy
    - (b) sturdiest
    - (c) sturdier
    - (d) very sturdy

19. The classroom is .... and full of freshness after the cleaning.
    - (a) brighter
    - (b) bright
    - (c) most bright
    - (d) more brighter

20. Our childhood years always seem .... to us.
    - (a) happy
    - (b) happiest
    - (c) more happy
    - (d) most happy

Directions (Q. Nos. 21-30) Complete the following paragraph by filling the most suitable adjective.

Everything was quite ......**(21)**..... here because this new job that I have got is .....**(22)**...... from any that I have had before. But I've gotten used to it now. After spending two years here, I am enjoying it even. I work as a finance manager and held mainly ......**(23)**..... for controlling the costs of the ongoing projects. I have got a ......**(24)**..... two bedroom flat, very similar to the one I had in Bengaluru. The only problem is the ......**(25)**..... and ......**(26)**..... sound of the ships from the harbor. The harbor is nearby, just one kilometer away from my place. I get woken very early by the loud noise of the ......**(27)**..... fishing trawlers coming from the sea with their ......**(28)**..... catch. The area is ......**(29)**..... for its variety of sea food and there are many ......**(30)**..... restaurants and malls nearby.

21. (a) new   (b) strange
    (c) brilliant   (d) different

22. (a) different   (b) old
    (c) anxious   (d) difficult

23. (a) responsible   (b) reliable
    (c) report   (d) no word needed

24. (a) decent   (b) nice
    (c) wonderful   (d) All of these

25. (a) pleasant   (b) cheerful
    (c) horrible   (d) Jolly

26. (a) soft   (b) loud
    (c) whispering   (d) louder

27. (a) giant   (b) full
    (c) hot   (d) fewer

28. (a) gradable   (b) main
    (c) huge   (d) three

29. (a) more famous
    (b) famous
    (c) infamous
    (d) not famous

30. (a) better   (b) best
    (c) good   (d) famous

2 Marks Questions

31. Find the correct usage of word 'long' in the given sentences.

A. He sat at the head of the long dining table with his three daughters on his left.

B. The other was white, with more longest golden curls.

C. It was the world's longest bridge.

D. It would be a most longer journey and a dangerous one.

Codes

(a) Only A   (b) Both A and C

(c) Only D   (d) Both B and D

32. Fill in the blanks with the suitable forms of the word BAD.

Abhay said to me, 'I know I do .... in maths, but at least I'm not the .... , there are several others who are .... than me in this subject.

1. worse, worst, badly
2. badly, worse, worst
3. badly, worst, worse
4. worst, worse, badly

(a) Only 1   (b) Both 2 and 3

(c) Only 3   (d) Both 1 and 4

33. Choose the sentence(s) with correct adjective order.

A. I love that really big old green antique car that is always parked at the end of the street.

B. My friend adopted a, big white beautiful bulldog.

C. We took a ride on a chinese, old, blue bus.

D. I have something that belongs to my grandmother. It is a small, square, metal vase.

Codes

(a) Only A   (b) Only B

(c) Both A and D   (d) Both A and B

34. Choose the right option to identify the kind of adjective underlined.

The script of this language has thousands of complex characters; some people think it is the most difficult language in the world.

(a) Thousands- adjective of quality, some – numerical adjective

(b) Thousands- numerical adjective, some- comparative adjective

(c) Thousands- numerical adjective, some- adjective of quantity

(d) Thousands- superlative adjective, some- demonstrative adjective

35. Replace the underlined word with a suitable word. Becca is wearing a lofty dress for the function tonight. Everyone agrees, it is a hugest dress.

P. Ugly, Huge

Q. Glittery, Beautiful

R. Glitter, Ugly

S. Ugly, Beautiful

Codes

(a) Only P   (b) Only Q

(c) Both P and R   (d) All of these

36. Choose the sentence that has the correct use of adjective.

I. My mother has a tiny, beautifully carved round jewelry box.

II. It is dusty and dark working in the mines.

III. Today is a spring day cool and crisp.

IV. He bought a decent white shirt from the supermarket.

Codes

(a) Only I

(b) Only III

(c) Both I and IV

(d) Both II and IV

Chapter 06

Articles

1 Mark Questions

Directions (Q. Nos. 1-5) Identify the articles in the sentences given below.

1. I want to try the exercises for advanced students. Can you please suggest me some?

   (a) to   (b) want (c) the   (d) for

2. She never calls back when someone leaves her a message.

   (a) Back   (b) leaves
   (c) what   (d) a

3. He returned from his Maths tuition almost an hour late.

   (a) he   (b) an
   (c) hour   (d) from

4. Do you know there is an institution for the blind people in this city?

   (a) Do, is   (b) an, the
   (c) this, know   (d) institution

5. I got my first job, when I was fourteen, as a dog walker.

   (a) a   (b) I   (c) got   (d) as

Directions (Q. Nos. 6-13) Fill in the blanks with appropriate articles.

6. I think there is some butter in .... fridge.

   (a) the   (b) little
   (c) an   (d) a

7. I used my shoe as .... hammer.

   (a) a
   (b) an
   (c) the
   (d) my

8. Have you fed .... dogs?

   (a) some   (b) the
   (c) few   (d) a

9. I am .... oldest in my family.

   (a) the   (b) a
   (c) that   (d) an

10. Who invented .... radio?

    (a) the   (b) this
    (c) a   (d) that

11. We went to .... same school.

    (a) some   (b) the
    (c) a   (d) that

12. My brother is going out with .... Chinese girl.

    (a) any   (b) a
    (c) an   (d) some

13. .... Dead sea lies 430.5 metres below the sea level.

    (a) A
    (b) An
    (c) The
    (d) No article

Direction (Q. Nos. 14-25) Complete the story by selecting the most appropriate answer from the options given below.

The afternoon was hot and so was ....**(14)**.... . ....**(15)**.... stop was at Templecombe nearly ....**(16)**.... ahead. In the carriage were ....**(17)**.... girl and a small boy. Aunt of ....**(18)**.... sat in ....**(19)**.... seat and in ....**(20)**..... corner seat on ....**(21)**..... side was a man who was a stranger to them but ....**(22)**..... and the small boy were ....**(23)**..... who fitted the compartment. .....**(24)**..... chattered on and on to their aunt like .....**(25)**..... that refuses to be put off. Most of the aunt's remarks seemed to begin with "Don't" and nearly all of the children's remarks began with "Why?"

14. (a) a railway carriage
    (b) the railway carriage
    (c) the railway carriages
    (d) a railway carriages

15. (a) The next   (b) A next
    (c) Next   (d) That next

16. (a) the hour   (b) hour
    (c) an hour   (d) a hour

17. (a) that small   (b) this small
    (c) the small   (d) a small

18. (a) a children   (b) children
    (c) child   (d) the children

19. (a) the corner   (b) a corner
    (c) that corner   (d) this corner

20. (a) a farther   (b) farther
    (c) the farther   (d) that farther

21. (a) the opposite   (b) an opposite
    (c) opposite   (d) a opposite

22. (a) a small girl   (b) this small girl
    (c) that small girl (d) the small girl

23. (a) ones   (b) those ones
    (c) that ones   (d) the ones

24. (a) Children   (b) Those children
    (c) The children   (d) These children

25. (a) the housefly   (b) a housefly
    (c) that housefly   (d) this housefly

2 Marks Questions

26. Choose the sentence that shows the incorrect use of articles.
    A. I studied the French in High school.
    B. He is good at a Maths.
    C. Creativity is a valuable quality.
    D. He swam to an island.
    Codes
    (a) Only B   (b) Only C
    (c) Both A and B   (d) Both B and D

27. Choose the sentence with the correct use of article from the following.
    A. I desperately need vacation.
    B. I am sure she will not return within an hour.
    C. Moon is very bright tonight.
    D. You should tell the police.
    Codes
    (a) Only A   (b) Both B and D
    (c) Only C   (d) Only D

28. Choose the suitable combination of articles to complete the sentence.
    Hey! You have been sitting at (i) .... computer all day. I think you should really take (ii) .... break now.
    (i) (a) A   (b) the
         (c) a   (d) the
    (ii) (a) the   (b) a
         (c) an   (d) No word

29. Check whether the articles underlined in the given sentence are used correctly or not. If not, replace them with suitable articles from the options.

Yesterday, I bought a blouse and (1) <u>the</u> shirt. The blouse was surprisingly cheap, but (2) <u>a</u> shirt was more expensive.

(a) (1) the, (2) an　　(b) (1) a, (2) the
(c) (1) the, (2) the　　(d) (1) a, (2) a

30. Fill in the blanks with the suitable articles to make a meaningful sentence.
My mother is .... English teacher and I am .... student studying in .... same school where my mother teaches.

(a) an, a, the　　　　(b) a, the, an
(c) the, a, an　　　　(d) an, the, a

31. In the sentences below, some words are numbered 1 to 4. Find out which word is wrongly used.
I like Japan. When I **1** fly to Japan, I usually fly to **2** the Narita International Airport. The last time I was in Japan, I climbed **3** the Mount Fuji. It was fun. **4** The Japanese people like to eat fish and rice.

(a) 1　　　　　　　(b) 2
(c) 3　　　　　　　(d) 4

32. Choose the sentence(s) with correct usage of articles.

A. I want to be an engineer when 1 grow up, but my father wants me to be a doctor.
B. My daughter is learning to play the guitar at her school.
C. Today, a inspector came to our school to visit.
D. It was Mary who Alex gave a keys to.

Codes
(a) Only D　　　　(b) Only B
(c) Both A and C　　(d) Both A and B

33. Consider the following statements.
1. The higher you throw the ball, the longer it will take to come back.
2. I had such a extraordinary dream last night.
3. That is an odd way to whistle.

Which of these statements is/are correct?

(a) 2 and 3　　　　(b) 1 and 3
(c) 1 and 2　　　　(d) All of these

34. Match the following to make meaningful sentences.

List I		List II	
A.	I bought an umbrella	1.	learning martial arts.
B.	Our neighbours have	2.	from Central Mall.
C.	I have an interest in	3.	jeans only yesterday.
D.	She bought a pair of	4.	two birds and a fish.

Codes

	A	B	C	D			A	B	C	D
(a)	3	1	2	4		(b)	1	4	3	2
(c)	2	4	1	3		(d)	3	2	4	1

35. Match the following.

List I		List II	
A.	A	1.	Terrible day at office
B.	The	2.	Middle class
C.	An	3.	Honorable discharge of duties

Codes

	A	B	C
(a)	1	2	3
(b)	2	3	1
(c)	3	1	2
(d)	2	1	3

Chapter 07

Prepositions

1 Mark Questions

Directions (Q. Nos. 1-7) Identify the prepositions in the following sentences by selecting the correct option.

1. My best friend John is named after his great-grandfather.
   (a) after   (b) my
   (c) is   (d) best

2. Grandpa stayed up until two in the morning.
   (a) stayed   (b) the
   (c) until   (d) two

3. I was visiting my best friend in the hospital.
   (a) was   (b) my
   (c) in   (d) visiting

4. He usually travels to Philadelphia by train.
   (a) by
   (b) he
   (c) usually
   (d) travels

5. You frequently see this kind of violence in films.
   (a) see   (b) this
   (c) violence   (d) in

6. I'll see you at home when I get there.
   (a) there   (b) get
   (c) at   (d) I

7. It has been snowing since Christmas morning.
   (a) since   (b) morning
   (c) it   (d) snowing

Directions (Q. Nos. 8-14) Fill in the blanks with appropriate prepositions.

8. Look .... this painting.
   (a) in   (b) before
   (c) at   (d) onto

9. .... the painting, you can see a little girl.
   (a) From (b) In   (c) At   (d) By

10. My grandma once owned the painting, but she gave it to me on my birthday. So it is a present .... my grandma.
    (a) about   (b) of
    (c) from   (d) through

11. I discussed the problem .... my teacher.
    (a) of   (b) with
    (c) since   (d) until

12. My uncle knows interesting facts .... the world's oceans.
    (a) over   (b) about
    (c) on   (d) to

13. He is worthy .... praise.
    (a) at   (b) of   (c) for   (d) since

14. Hard work is the key .... success.
   (a) in   (b) to
   (c) on   (d) into

Directions (Q. Nos. 15-22) Replace the underlined words with suitable prepositions from the given options.

15. Most people agree <u>at</u> the fact that kindergarten greatly contributes <u>on</u> a child's mental development.
   (a) to, towards   (b) in, to
   (c) on, upon   (d) by, with

16. Although he studied hard, he couldn't succeed <u>to</u> getting a high score <u>for</u> his test.
   (a) at, in   (b) in, in
   (c) for, of   (d) by, for

17. There are different sets <u>in</u> language learning sets available <u>at</u> all age groups.
   (a) of, for   (b) at, upto
   (c) at, for   (d) upto, in

18. All the candidates are looking forward <u>by</u> the announcement <u>into</u> our test scores.
   (a) for, to   (b) of, to
   (c) to, of   (d) about, of

19. Since I am busy preparing <u>at</u> the exam which is tomorrow, I can't go <u>to</u> with you tonight.
   (a) with, in   (b) for, out
   (c) of, in   (d) in, out

20. The students walk five kilometers to school, so they need <u>for</u> get up very early <u>on</u> the morning.
   (a) with, at
   (b) to, in
   (c) for, in
   (d) to, no word

21. As my school was <u>far</u> to my house, I used to come home <u>from</u> lunch time.
   (a) in, for   (b) next, during
   (c) at, within   (d) for, for

22. I was born <u>at</u> 23rd <u>in</u> April, so there is no school when it's my birthday.
   (a) in, of   (b) on, off
   (c) of, in   (d) on, of

Directions (Q. Nos. 23-29) Complete the story by filling in suitable prepositions from the options given below.

Mr. Sharma is a careless driver. ....**(23)**.... he has a reputation of being a dangerous driver. The police has fined him four times ......**(24)**...... speeding. Since he drives carelessly, his wife usually drives when the children are ......**(25)**...... them. The children often feel sick ......**(26)**...... the car. When this happens, Mrs Sharma has ......**(27)**...... stop the car .....**(28)**...... them to have a break. Then she has to drive .....**(29)**....... the forest road to get some fresh air.

23. (a) infact   (b) to
     (c) for   (d) of

24. (a) for   (b) of
     (c) to   (d) off

25. (a) by   (b) for
     (c) along   (d) with

26. (a) into   (b) in
     (c) behind   (d) towards

27. (a) to   (b) at
     (c) off   (d) beyond

28. (a) for   (b) from
     (c) due to   (d) near

29. (a) in   (b) out
     (c) along   (d) inside

2 Marks Questions

30. Choose the incorrect option from the following.

I. My uncle deals in spices and condiments.

II. The teacher stressed on the importance of planning.

III. Reni stormed below the hall in anger.

IV. Tomatoes are rich in antioxidants and good for health.

Codes

(a) Both I and II   (b) Only III
(c) Both III and IV   (d) Only II

31. Replace the words in bold with suitable prepositions.

Changes in our society **before** recent years have weakened family life. A generation ago, most houses got **off** on Dad's paycheck and mom stayed home. Families used to eat together, talk **to** each other while eating and a healthy interaction was seen.

(a) in, by, with
(b) after, along, among
(c) on, of, between
(d) No change

32. Fill in the blanks with correct order of the propositions.

The giant elephant was lucky .... return .... the shed .... a violent storm .... getting hurt.

(a) without, to, from, in
(b) to, without, in, from
(c) to, in, from, without
(d) from, to, without, in

33. Consider the following statements.

1. The salesman failed to interest me in any of his products.

2. His bodyguards protect him with potential harm.

Which of these statement is/are correct?

(a) Only 1   (b) Only 2
(c) Both 1 and 2   (d) None of these

34. Choose the option having the correct use of prepositions.

A. Rita is going towards the seminar.
B. The cat jumped inside the pond.
C. She was completely overcome with joy.
D. I love the verses from 'Macbeth'.

Codes

(a) Only A   (b) Both A and C
(c) Only D   (d) Both C and D

Directions (Q. No. 35) Given below are two statements marked as Assertion(A) and Reason (R). Read both the statements carefully and choose the correct option from the following.

35. Assertion (A) Preposition of direction tells the readers about the direction in which something or someone is moving.

Reason (R) Preposition of direction describes a direction between two nouns, e.g. Arun sat near the campfire. Here, we know about the direction in which Arun sat (close to) the campfire.

Codes

(a) Both A and R are true and R is the correct explanation of A
(b) Both A and R are true, but R is not the correct explanation of A
(c) A is true, but R is false
(d) A is false, but R is true

36. Fill in the blank with the correct prepositional phrase.

That book, ..., is a favorite among students as it is always on top of the reservation list in the library.

1. by a tattered cover
2. under a tattered cover
3. with a tattered cover
4. with the tattered cover

(a) Only 1   (b) Only 2
(c) Only 3   (d) Only 4

Conjunctions

1 Mark Questions

Directions (Q. Nos. 1-7) Identify the conjunctions in the sentences given below.

1. Despite being very rich, he never shows off.
   (a) rich   (b) Despite
   (c) shows   (d) very

2. I am not feeling well; however, I will come to the party.
   (a) to   (b) however
   (c) feeling   (d) come

3. Although I have had my lunch, my hunger has not gone.
   (a) Although   (b) gone
   (c) my   (d) has

4. You shouldn't go out because it's raining heavily.
   (a) you   (b) go
   (c) because   (d) it's

5. My mother and I went to the market for shopping.
   (a) my   (b) the
   (c) to   (d) and

6. Please come on time, otherwise we may miss the flight.
   (a) otherwise
   (b) come
   (c) flight
   (d) miss

7. I will give you my car provided you come back before 5 o'clock.
   (a) before   (b) back
   (c) give   (d) provided

Directions (Q. Nos. 8-14) Fill in the blanks by selecting the most appropriate conjunctions from the options given below.

8. This old woman spoke .... English .... Russian.
   (a) either, nor   (b) neither, nor
   (c) only, but   (d) although, yet

9. She tried to learn English .... it was too difficult.
   (a) and   (b) but
   (c) so   (d) since

10. Last night I went to sleep .... I was very tired.
    (a) since   (b) for
    (c) and   (d) so

11. We have tickets for the cinema .... the opera.
    (a) yet   (b) and
    (c) or   (d) nor

12. Would you like orange juice .... cola?
    (a) and   (b) or
    (c) but   (d) since

13. This is Mary. She is very rich .... unhappy.

(a) and   (b) but   (c) so   (d) or

14. She is good at Maths .... her favourite subject is History.

(a) or   (b) but
(c) so   (d) and

Directions (Q. Nos. 15-21) Given below is a paragraph which has some blanks. Complete the paragraph by filling in suitable conjunction from the options given below the passage.

Wildlife refers to all animals .....**(15)**..... other living things that exist in the wilderness. Long ago, primitive man started domesticating animals as pets .....**(16)**..... growing plants to produce food. Much has changed .....**(17)**..... he began controlling them .....**(18)**...... using them for his own benefit. ......**(19)**..... some of the changes are positive, many of them are negative. ......**(20)**..... the mid-20th century there has been an increase in the average temperature of air near the Earth's surface ......**(21)**...... oceans because of human interference.

Options

15. (a) and   (b) but
   (c) or   (d) both

16. (a) and   (b) but
   (c) or   (d) since

17. (a) but   (b) and
   (c) since   (d) or

18. (a) and   (b) or
   (c) but   (d) because

19. (a) Since   (b) But
   (c) Because   (d) Although

20. (a) While   (b) Since
   (c) Because   (d) But

21. (a) or   (b) but
   (c) and   (c) since

22. In this sentence 'not only, but also' are which type of conjuction.
   She ate not only biryani but also dessert.

(a) Coordinating   (b) Subordinating
(c) Correlative   (d) Compound

Directions (Q. Nos. 23-27) Fill in the blanks by selecting the appropriate conjunctions from the options given below.

23. ....somewhat annoying, she was quite an interesting character .... friendly too.

(a) Unless, or   (b) Since, as
(c) Though, and   (d) Because, and

24. Never start an argument .... you know you are right. .... you are right, try to avoid it

(a) unless, even if
(b) because, even then
(c) since, but
(d) when, because

25. The offer was .... tempting .... I just could not decline it.

(a) so, that   (b) neither, nor
(c) either, or   (d) not only, but also

26. We could reschedule the meeting .... you would prefer that .... we can cancel it altogether.

(a) unless, if   (b) if, or
(c) when, though   (d) where, and

27. She knows that you went to the movies .... she found the tickets .... the parking slip of M2K mall.

(a) unless, until
(b) until, unless
(c) because, besides
(d) after, before

2 Marks Questions

28. State True or False for the following statements. T stands for True and F stands for False.

1. The thieves entered the house soon after the family went to bed.
2. There is a test today since the teacher has forgotten about it.

(a) 1-T,2-F   (b) 1-F,2-T
(c) 1-F,2-F   (d) 1-T,2-T

29. Choose the option that has right usage of the words given in bold.

A. We had to wait fifteen minutes for the shop to open **since** we had arrived early.
B. The ski slopes were busy **since** the cold freezing weather.
C. We couldn't go out because he has asked us to wait **until** he returned.
D. The soldiers marched **unless** the sergeant shouted his orders.

Codes
(a) Both A and C   (b) Only D
(c) Both B and D   (d) Only C

30 Choose the sentence with incorrect use of conjunctions from the following.

A. It is very sunny today that's why I am wearing sunglasses.
B. Mudit did his homework very hurriedly because he didn't make any mistakes.
C. Anil watched the Cricket match whereas his country was playing.
D. Although the test was very difficult, all the students got one hundred per cent.

Codes
(a) Only B   (b) Only A
(c) Both B and C   (d) Both A and D

31. Select one conjunction that can be filled in all the blanks.

I. I have to go to work at 9, ... I'm waking up at 7 AM.
II. Ravi doesn't like to drive, ... he takes cab everywhere.
III. He's honest............. everyone trusts him.
IV. I know you must be tired, ... I will let you take rest.

Codes
(a) and   (b) so
(c) or   (d) since

32. Replace the word in *Italics* to make the sentence meaningful.

An International Committee issued a depressing forecast of how human beings *or* natural ecosystems will be influenced in the future; *meanwhile* the effects of global warming intensify.

(a) and, as soon as   (b) or, however
(c) and, as   (d) and, conversely

33. Read the sentence carefully and find out the conjunction that is not placed properly.

1. When they entered the house, they found that it had been ransacked, nothing
2. even though was missing; they called the police
3. and reported about this incident.

(a) when
(b) even though
(c) and
(d) no error in placing

34. Choose the word that is most suitable for joining these sentences.

1. He is already a good performer.
2. Nobody can question his eligibility anymore.

A. since   B. despite
C. whenever   D. because
(a) Only A   (b) Only B
(c) Both A and B   (d) Both C and D

Tenses

1 Mark Questions

Directions (Q. Nos. 1-7) Choose the correct answer from the given options based on the verb given in brackets.

1. Dr Francis is one of those professors who .... distracted most of the time. (seem)
   (a) seem　　　　　(b) seems
   (c) is seem　　　　(d) was seem

2. Neither Luis nor his parents .... the least bit interested in keeping in touch with her. (is)
   (a) is　　　　　(b) am
   (c) are　　　　(d) was

3. Everyone in this team .... really hard to please the new coach. (try)
   (a) tried
   (b) try
   (c) tries
   (d) was tried

4. Mr Bradley, alongwith his two sisters, ... lived in this town for thirty years. (has)
   (a) have　　　　(b) had
   (c) has　　　　(d) is

5. Keep the food covered or the flies .... it. (contaminate)
   (a) contaminates　　(b) contaminated
   (c) contaminate　　(d) will contaminate

6. The price of these jeans was reasonable, so I .... it. (buy)
   (a) buy　　　　(b) bought
   (c) had bought　　(d) will bought

7. None of my friends .... there. (is)
   (a) am　　　　(b) was
   (c) are　　　　(d) were

Directions (Q. Nos. 8-17) Read the sentences given below and figure out the correct tense that fits in.

8. He .... a cellphone.
   (a) has　　　　　(b) is having
   (b) Both (a) and (b)　(d) None of these

9. I .... you are wrong.
   (a) thinking
   (b) am thinking
   (c) Both (a) and (b)
   (d) None of the above

10. I .... his letter a week ago.
    (a) received
    (b) have received
    (c) Both (a) and (b)
    (d) None of the above

11. I .... my salary to CRY.
    (a) gives
    (b) have/had given
    (c) Both (a) and (b)
    (d) None of the above

12. I .... here for hours.
   (a) have stood
   (b) have been standing
   (c) Both (a) and (b)
   (d) were

13. Ajit .... the ball to Mohinder who .... it past the goalkeeper.
   (a) passed, had kicked
   (b) is passing, has kicked
   (c) was passing, is kicking
   (d) None of the above

14. The Headmaster .... to speak to you.
   (a) wants   (b) is wanting
   (b) Both (a) and (b)   (d) None of these

15. Here are your shoes; I .... them.
   (a) just cleaned
   (b) have just cleaned
   (c) Both (a) and (b)
   (d) None of the above

16. Humans .... to end violence and conflicts up to now, but maybe they will find a way in the future.
   (a) had never managed
   (b) have never managed
   (c) Both (a) and (b)
   (d) None of the above

17. We .... for his call since 4.20 pm.
   (a) are waiting
   (b) have been waiting
   (c) Both (a) and (b)
   (d) None of the above

Directions (Q. Nos. 18-20) Fill in the blanks by choosing appropriate option to complete the sentences.

18. Make sure you .... the electricity before you .... mending the light switch.

   (a) are disconnecting, ere starting
   (b) disconnect, start
   (c) will disconnect, started
   (d) disconnect, you have started

19. Ashok bravely .... the attack .... as a brave soldier.
   (a) have withstood, fight
   (b) withstood, fighting
   (c) had withstood, fought
   (d) All of the above

20. Most people .... being disturbed while they ....
   (a) don't like, are working
   (b) would like, worked
   (c) like, worked
   (d) never liked, are working

Directions (Q. Nos. 21-27) Fill in the blanks and complete the passage by choosing the most appropriate option.

Anita is giving her colleague some advice about a journey she is planning.

Anita Ok, well, as you haven't done this trip before I ....(21)...... give you a few tips to save your time. First you ....(22)....... make sure you get to the airport really early because you always ....(23)...... stand in a queue for ages to check in. They really ....(24)....... introduce a more efficient system, but they won't. Anyway, then you ....(25)...... go through passport control. You should take something good to read because you ....(26)...... quite a long wait in the departure lounge. At least you ....(27)....... be able to sit down there.

21. (a) had better   (b) would like to
   (c) should   (d) shall

22. (a) should   (b) may
   (c) ought to   (d) can

23. (a) have to   (b) need to
   (c) must   (d) could

24. (a) should   (b) might
(c) can   (d) must

25. (a) had to   (b) will have to
(c) have to   (d) must

26. (a) had better   (b) will have
(c) had been   (d) have

27. (a) ought to   (b) should
(c) may not   (d) should not

2 Marks Questions

28. Replace the words in Italics with the correct form of tenses given in the options.

There *are* many people at the funeral. They *come* to pay their respects to the deceased. One of the guests *had given* a small envelope that probably contained some money. It was so thoughtful of that guest.

(a) were, come, gave
(b) are, have come, had given
(c) were, had come, had given
(d) are, have come, given

29. Find the correct sentence from the following.

A. When I was reaching the station, the train had started.
B. Some of the cargo had been damaged by the sea water.

(a) Only A   (b) Only B
(c) Both A and B   (d) None of these

30. Find the error in the following sentence.
I **had lots** of different jobs when **I was a** teenager; I **worked as a** waiter and as a shop attendant at one of the local bakery shop.

(a) had lots of   (b) I was a
(c) worked as a   (d) No error

31. Choose the grammatically correct sentence from the following.

A. She have met him when she was in Jaipur.
B. He seems to be enjoying his stay at Mahabaleswar.

C. I can't give you a lift, my car broken down.
D. I am working here for twenty years next April.

Codes
(a) Only A   (b) Both A and D
(c) Both B and C   (d) Only B

32. Find the incorrect sentence from the following.

A. The Sun rise in the East.
B. There aren't many students in the library.
C. She gave a cookie to each child
D. I haven't got any pictures in my room.

Codes
(a) Only B   (b) Only A
(c) Both C and D   (d) Both B and C

33. Choose the option that uses past continuous form of verb.

A. I waited for an hour at the theatre.
B. I was waiting for him last night.
C. He had been waiting for this moment only.
D. You were watching TV last night.

Codes
(a) Only A   (b) Both A and C
(c) Both B and D   (d) Only D

34. Choose the continuous or simple form of verb in brackets to fill in the gap.
The accident happened at one of the mountain passes when they .... (come) down the Mount Everest.

A. came   B. were coming
C. are coming   D. None of these
(a) Only A   (b) Both B and C
(c) Only B   (d) All of these

Chapter 10

Active and Passive Voice

1 Mark Questions

Directions (Q. Nos. 1-5) Change these sentences from active to passive voice. Fill in the blanks by choosing the correct option from the given choices.

1. *Active* People speak Portuguese in Brazil.

   Passive Portuguese .... in Brazil.
   - (a) is speak
   - (b) is spoke
   - (c) is spoken
   - (d) speak

2. *Active* People see this beach as the most beautiful in the country.

   Passive This beach .... as the most beautiful in the country.
   - (a) is seen
   - (b) is saw
   - (c) is see
   - (d) sees

3. *Active* A friend gave me this sweater.
   Passive This sweater .... to me by a friend.
   - (a) is given
   - (b) was gave
   - (c) was given
   - (d) gave

4. *Active* A famous author wrote these letters.

   Passive These letters .... by a famous author.
   - (a) is written
   - (b) were written
   - (c) has been written
   - (d) were wrote

5. *Active* Who taught you how to write Hindi?

   Passive By whom were .... how to write Hindi?
   - (a) you teach
   - (b) taught you
   - (c) you teach
   - (d) you taught

Directions (Q. Nos. 6-8) Replace the underlined words to complete the sentences in passive voice.

6. By the time the manager arrived, the problem <u>is solved</u>.
   - (a) has already solved
   - (b) had already been solved
   - (c) was already solved
   - (d) were already being solved

7. Mr Green <u>is awarded</u> for his commendable services to the university.
   - (a) has been awarded
   - (b) was awarded
   - (c) awarded
   - (d) have been awarded

8. A new book <u>is being published</u> by the company next year.
   - (a) will publish
   - (b) will be published
   - (c) would publish
   - (d) will have to publish

Directions (Q. Nos. 9-15) Read the newspaper report and put the verbs in brackets in the correct passive forms. Choose from the options given below the report.

The 'VIRAT' ship, one of India's most popular tourist attractions ....**(9)**...... (*devastate*) by a fire which police think might ....**(10)**...... (*start*) on purpose. More than 40 fire fighters ......**(11)**....... (*call*) to save the 138 year-old tea-clipper ship in Mumbai early on Monday morning.

A spokesman for the Mumbai fire service said the whole ship ....**(12)**...... (*affect*) by the massive fire but nobody was hurt. The police do not know as of yet what caused the fire but said they were treating it as suspicious. That means the fire may ....**(13)**...... (*start*) on purpose rather than by accident.

Dinesh Dutta, from the group which looks after the ship, said the fire was a significant setback but they were determined to put the ship back again. He said the decks could not ....**(14)**..... (*save*) but the damage did not appear as bad as first feared.

Half the planking as well as the old artefacts on board escaped the damage as they ....**(15)**...... (*remove*)   while   the refurbishing was under way.

He added "She's been through storms and hurricanes. She's been battling all her life. She's not dead yet, far from it."

9. (a) has been devastated
   (b) is being devastated
   (c) was devastated
   (d) was been devastated

10. (a) had started
    (b) have been started
    (c) was started
    (d) started

11. (a) has been called
    (b) was called
    (c) were called
    (d) had called

12. (a) had been affected
    (b) was affected
    (c) is affected
    (d) was being affected

13. (a) have been started
    (b) had started
    (c) has been started
    (d) started

14. (a) be saved
    (b) have been saved
    (c) has been saved
    (d) were being saved

15. (a) have been removed
    (b) were being removed
    (c) had been removed
    (d) had removed

Directions (Q. Nos. 16-26) Study the flow chart below. Write a description of the process of recycling plastic in passive voice by filling in the blanks in the boxes by selecting the correct options from those given below.

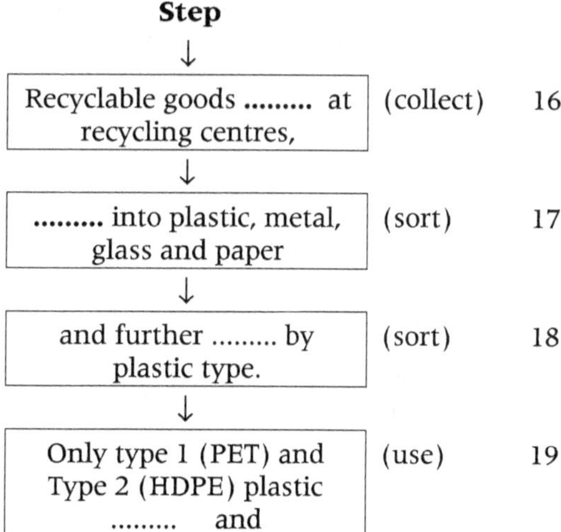

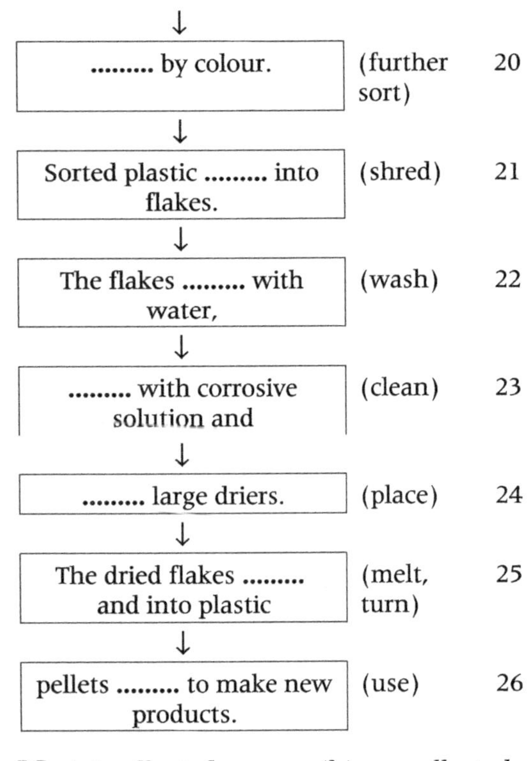

16. (a) collected   (b) are collected
(c) can be collect   (d) were collected

17. (a) sorted
(b) sort
(c) are being sorted
(d) were sorted

18. (a) are sorted   (b) being sorted
(c) will be sorted   (d) sorted

19. (a) are used   (b) were being used
(c) are being used   (d) will be used

20. (a) further sorted
(b) were further sorted
(c) are being further sorted
(d) will be further sorted

21. (a) are shredded
(b) were shreddred
(c) is shredded
(d) were being shredded

22. (a) are washed
(b) were washed
(c) were being washed
(d) will be washed

23. (a) cleaned
(b) will be cleaned
(c) were being cleaned
(d) was being cleaned

24. (a) are placed in   (b) placed in
(c) to be placed in   (d) were placed in

25. (a) are melted, turned
(b) were being melted, turned
(c) are being melted, turned
(d) melted, turned

26. (a) use
(b) used
(c) are used
(d) None of the above

2 Marks Questions

27. Choose the option that is the correct changeover of Active voice into Passive voice.
The employees brought up this issue during the meeting.

A. This issue was brought up by the employees during the meeting.
B. This issue has been brought up by the employees during the meeting.
C. This issue is brought up by the employees during the meeting.
D. This issue would brought up by the employees during the meeting.

Codes
(a) Only B   (b) Only A
(c) Both A and D   (d) Both C and D

28. Choose the option that is the correct changeover of Passive voice into Active voice.
He was told by the professor not to talk in the class.

A. The professor tell him not to talk in the class.

B. The professor is telling him not to talk in the class.

C. The professor told him not to talk in the class.

D. The professor was telling him not to talk in the class.

Codes

(a) Only C   (b) Both A and C

(c) Both B and D   (d) Any of these

29. Identify the correct form of verb in the following sentence when it will be changed to passive voice.

The government spends lot of money in building rehabilitation centers for drug addicts.

(i) is spent

(ii) spent

(iii) had spend

(iv) had been spending

(a) Only (i)

(b) Only (ii)

(c) Both(iii) and (iv)

(d) None of the above

30. Find the correct voice changeover to the sentence given below.

People generally assume that fat people are lazy.

A. Fat people are assumed generally to be lazy.

B. It is assumed that fat people are lazy.

C. Fat people are generally assumed to be lazy.

D. Fat people have been assumed to be lazy.

Codes

(a) Only A   (b) Both B and C

(c) Only C   (d) Only D

31. Replace the bold words by the most suitable words to make a proper sentence in passive voice.

New, disease resistant trees **have been bringing** back the splendor of what **had been call** one of the prettiest towns in France.

(a) had been bringing, have been called

(b) has been bringing, has been called

(c) are bringing, had been called

(d) are bringing, have been called

32. Complete the blank to frame a sentence in passive voice properly.

A poll on how many women seek healthcare facilities for childbirth .... (conduct) by me for my year end project in my neighbourhood; this .... (mean) I .... (interview) my neighbours in their homes.

(a) were conducted, means, interviewed

(b) was conducted, meant, was interviewing

(c) is conducted, meant, may interview

(d) are conducted, meant, was interviewing

Chapter 11

Direct and Indirect Speech

1 Mark Questions

Directions (Q. Nos. 1-6) Complete the sentences by choosing the most appropriate option.

1. "I have no idea ...."
   - (a) where she's
   - (b) where she is
   - (c) where is she
   - (d) where would she

2. "Could you tell me .... gone?"
   - (a) where she's
   - (b) where is she
   - (c) where has she
   - (d) where was she

3. I asked them where .... going.
   - (a) were they
   - (b) are they
   - (c) they were
   - (d) is they

4. "Can you tell me how much .... cost?"
   - (a) will it
   - (b) does it
   - (c) it will
   - (d) it does

5. "Do you have any idea how long .... me to do it?"
   - (a) did it take
   - (b) it took
   - (c) took it
   - (d) that has taken

6. She asked me where .... from.
   - (a) do I came
   - (b) came I
   - (c) I came
   - (d) I did come

Directions (Q. Nos. 7-12) Given below are sentences in Direct Speech. Out of the four options suggested, select the one which best expresses the same sentence in Indirect Speech.

7. He said to her, "Are you coming to the party?"
   - (a) He told her if she was coming to the party?
   - (b) He asked her if she was coming to the party.
   - (c) He asked her whether she would come to the party.
   - (d) He asked her if she will be coming to the party.

8. They said, "Mother, we are not hungry; we shall eat later."
   - (a) They told the mother they are not hungry, they will eat later.
   - (b) They told the mother that they were not hungry and would eat later.
   - (c) They said to the mother they shall eat later as they were not hungry.
   - (d) They informed the mother that they are not hungry and would eat later.

9. He said to his brother, "The Earth moves round the Sun".
   (a) He told his brother that the Earth moves round the Sun.
   (b) He told his brother that the Earth would move round the Sun.
   (c) He told his brother that the Earth moved round the Sun.
   (d) He told his brother that the Earth had moved round the Sun.

10. He said to me, "Are you going to Jaipur?"
    (a) He told me if I am going to Jaipur?
    (b) He said to me if I was going to Jaipur.
    (c) He asked me if I was going to Jaipur.
    (d) He asked me if I am going to Jaipur.

11. The boy said, "I saw him while I was running".
    (a) The boy said that he had seen him while he (the boy) was running.
    (b) The boy said that he had saw him while he was running.
    (c) The boy said that he had seen him while he had run.
    (d) The boy said that he did see him while running.

12. She said, "I saw a lion there".
    (a) She said that she saw a lion there.
    (b) She said that she had seen a lion there.
    (c) She told that she saw a lion there.
    (d) She said that she saw a lion here.

Directions (Q. Nos. 13-18) For each of the following indirect speech sentences, choose the best word or phrase to complete the blank from the options given.

13. Last week, our teachers told us that we .... a spelling test at the end of the week on Friday.
    (a) can have   (b) did have
    (c) would have   (d) had had

14. Three days ago a friend told me that she was going to visit me .... but she didn't come.
    (a) tomorrow   (b) the next day
    (c) the day before (d) next day

15. When I spoke to Bela yesterday, she said that she .... to a party the night before.
    (a) has went   (b) had gone
    (c) was going   (d) did go

16. On Tuesday, Anand told the teacher that he had missed the lesson .... as he was on leave.
    (a) yesterday   (b) before day
    (c) the day before (d) the before day

17. Last week Dinesh sent a leave application saying that he .... to school because of fever.
    (a) didn't come   (b) couldn't come
    (c) doesn't come   (d) wasn't come

18. When we asked her, Sushma told us that she .... a ghost before.
    (a) never saw   (b) never seen
    (c) had never seen (d) did never see

Directions (Q. Nos. 19-24) Change the following sentences into Direct narration. Choose from the options.

19. John said that he loved that town.
    (a) John said, "I will love this town".
    (b) John said, "I love this town".
    (c) John said, "I loved this town".
    (d) John said, "I am loving this town".

20. He asked me if I was sure that I liked soccer.
    (a) "Are you sure you like soccer?" He said to me.
    (b) "Were you sure, you liked soccer?" He told me.

(c) "Are you sure", He asked me.

(d) "Are you sure you are liking soccer?" He asked.

21. She asked him what he had decided to do.

(a) "What have you decided to do?" She said to him.

(b) "What do you want to do?" She asked him.

(c) "What did you want to do?" She asked him.

(d) "What will you do?" She asked.

22. He advised the students to revise their lessons.

(a) "You may revise your lessons," he said.

(b) "You should revise your lessons" he said.

(c) "you will revise your lessons"?, said he.

(d) "You can revise your lessons," he told.

23. He wanted to know where I was born.

(a) "Where was you born", he asked me.

(b) "Where is your birth from", he asked me.

(c) "Where were you born?" he asked me.

(d) "Where did you took birth?" he asked me.

24. He asked/advised me to be nice to my brother.

(a) He said, "Be nice to your brother."

(b) He told, "you should be nice to your brother."

(c) He said, "You have to be nice to your brother."

(d) He told, "you will have to be nice to your brother."

2 Marks Questions

25. Complete the given blank with correct alternative.

"When will you be visiting the hospital? I want to come along" she said.

She wanted to know when .... the hospital as she wanted to come along.

(a) I would be visit

(b) will visit

(c) I would be visiting

(d) will be visiting

26. Choose the incorrect option from the following sentences in reported speech.

A. Sam observed that is the time to leave.

B. He asked me why I am going to school.

C. Dad asks, where his clean shirt is?

D. Mom told him that it was hanging on the balcony.

Codes

(a) Only A   (b) Both C and D

(c) Only D   (d) Both B and C

27. Select the one which best expresses the same sentence in direct speech.

Top told Tip it was his turn to make the dinner that night.

A. Top said " it was your turn to make dinner tonight, Tip".

B. "It was your turn to make dinner tonight, Tip", said to Top.

C. "It was your turn to make dinner this night", said Top.

D. "It is your turn to make dinner tonight Tip", said Top.

Codes

(a) Only D   (b) Only B

(c) Both B and C   (d) Both A and D

28. Identify the option that rightly changes present indefinite tense in reporting speech to past indefinite tense in reported speech.

"They take exercises every day".

A. They said that they took exercises every day.

B. They say that they were taking exercises every day.

C. They said that have been taking exercises.

D. They said that they had taken exercises.

Codes

(a) Only B   (b) Only A

(c) Only C   (d) Only D

29. Replace the bold words with suitable words to make an appropriate sentence. Hari said to the Sales Clerk at the post office, "But you **charging** me ₹ 5 yesterday for a letter to Kanpur and this is only a short distance away, I think you **cheated** me so I will go to another post office."

(a) charged, are cheating

(b) were charging, have cheated

(c) charged, has cheated

(d) were charged, had cheated

30. Choose the correct option.

1. " Where was my red shirt hanged?", dad demanded.

2. " It have been hanging in the kitchen", replied mom.

3. "Why I could not see it earlier!" exclaimed dad.

Which of the following statement is correct?

Codes

(a) 1 and 2   (b) Only 3

(c) 2 and 3   (d) Only 2

Direction (Q.No. 31) Given below are two sentences marked as Assertion (A) and Reason (R). Read both the statements carefully and choose the correct option.

31. **Assertion** (A) He said," Sally do the exercise" will change to He told Sally to do the exercise: in reported speech.

Reason (R) When transforming questions in reported speech, we should check whether we need to change pronouns, tenses or the place.

Which is correct?

(a) Both A and R are true and R is the correct explanation of A

(b) Both A and R are true, but R is not the correct explanation of A

(c) A is true, but R is false

(d) A is false, but R is true

32. Match the following.

	List I		List II
A.	She said,"You are a brilliant student."	1.	She told him that he was a brilliant student.
B.	She said to him "You are a brilliant student."	2.	She said that all of us were brilliant students.
C.	She said to them "You are brilliant students."	3.	She told me that I was a brilliant student.
D.	She said "You all are brilliant student."	4.	She told them that they were brilliant students.

Codes

	A	B	C	D			A	B	C	D
(a)	1	2	4	3		(b)	2	4	1	3
(c)	4	3	2	1		(d)	3	1	4	2

Chapter 12

Error Detection

1 Mark Questions

Directions (Q. Nos. 1-5) Find the error in the following sentences.

1. Do you see that funny cloud, shape like a dog's head?
   (a) dog's   (b) shape
   (c) a   (d) like

2. Can I borrow that new pair of shoes you buy last week from the Central market?
   (a) buy   (b) that   (c) borrow (d) of

3. Just listen to me very carefully while I read in these amazing statistics.
   (a) read   (b) while
   (c) in   (d) these

4. I frankly told Gaurav yesterday that the new hairstyle is not suiting him.
   (a) frankly   (b) small
   (c) hairstyle   (d) is

5. The rock band wouldn't play very well last year, but now they are much better.
   (a) wouldn't   (b) play
   (c) but   (d) much

Directions (Q. Nos. 6-10) From the following sentences, find the sentence which has no error.

6. (a) There are four senior secondary schools in this town.
   (b) Their are four senior secondary school in this town.
   (c) There is four senior secondary schools within this town.
   (d) There is four secondary senior school in this town.

7. (a) His brother said that he is not gone to attend the college that day.
   (b) His brother told to me that he was not going to attend the college that day.
   (c) His brother said that he was not going to attend the college that day.
   (d) His brother asked to her that how he was not going to attend the college that day.

8. (a) People here are nice friendly straightforward honest and hard working.
   (b) People here are nice, friendly, straight forward, honest and hard working.
   (c) People here are nice, honest, straightforward, honest and hard working.
   (d) People here are nice, honest and straightforward, honest and hard working.

9. (a) Our manager takes a keen interest in the welfare of the staff.
   (b) Our manager take a keen interest in the welfare of the staff.
   (c) Our manager takes a genuine interest on the welfare of the staff.
   (d) Our manager take a keen interest for the welfare of its' staffs.

10. (a) It had been two months while our regular study began.
    (b) It have been two months unless our regular studies begins.
    (c) It has been two months until our regular studies begin.
    (d) It has been two months since our regular studies began.

Directions (Q. Nos. 11-15) Each sentence of this paragraph has an error. Find out the word/part that has an error.

A picnic is a kind of excursion that is arranged with family and friends on the scenic outdoors. Everyone gets together in a place, ideally a park or resort, and cook and eat lunch together, play games and spent a whole day making memories.

In tropical countries like India, families generally plan exciting picnics during winter holidays unless the weather remains largely pleasant during that time. These picnics has immense significance in our life. They allow us to take a break from our busy routine and spend time for our family.

11. (a) Picnic   (b) on
    (c) Scenic   (d) Arranged

12. (a) Spent   (b) Gets
    (c) Making   (d) Ideally

13. (a) Families   (b) During
    (c) Unless   (d) Largely

14. (a) Immense   (b) Has
    (c) These   (d) In

15. (a) Take   (b) Spend   (c) For   (d) From

2 Marks Questions

Directions (Q. Nos. 16-20) In the following statements, state true or false.

16. 1. Swimming in the sea in such rough conditions have to be a very difficult and a dangerous task.
    2. Swimming in the sea in such rough conditions must be a very difficult and a dangerous task.
    (a) 1-T, 2-F   (b) 1-F, 2-T
    (c) 1-T, 2-T   (d) 1-F, 2-F

17. 1. My dog would have jumped very high if he was younger.
    2. One of the boys was able to get inside that deep and dark cave.
    (a) 1-T, 2-F   (b) 1-F, 2-T
    (c) 1-T, 2-T   (d) 1-F, 2-F

18. 1. This is strictly between you and 1, the boss is not a good person.
    2. I wanted to talk to you yesterday, but you were engrossed in some work.
    3. Oh my God! The cheese is past its expiry date.

(a) 1-T, 2-F, 3-F   (b) 1-F, 2-T, 3-F
(c) 1-F, 2-T, T, 3-T   (d) All are true

19. 1. "l would like to thank everyone for this award". Said Victor.
    2. I had butter toast and eggs for breakfast.
    3. I took cakes and coffee to the beach to spend my evening there.
    (a) 1-T, 2-F, 3-F   (b) 1-F, 2-T, 3-F
    (c) All are false   (d) All are true

20. 1. I am a vegetarian and thankfully I love fruit and vegetable.
    2. I am sure Nira will be able to explain everything when she returns.
    3. It was he who came running into the room a short while ago.
    4. Rumors are that they might leave the country very soon.
    (a) All are true
    (b) All are false
    (c) 1 is false, rest is true
    (d) 2 is false, rest is true

Sentence Arrangement

1 Mark Questions

Directions (Q. Nos. 1-4) In the questions below, the four parts of a sentence are given in jumbled form. Select the option so that a meaningful sentence is formed.

1. A. I had expected
   B. the performance of our players
   C. worse than
   D. was
   (a) BACD (b) BDCA (c) DCAB (d) CDAB

2. A. were all shocked
   B. at his failure
   C. they
   D. in the competition
   (a) BCDA (b) CBDA (c) CABD (d) DCAB

3. A. as my behaviour
   B. I need not offer any explanation
   C. regarding this incident
   D. is self-explanatory
   (a) ACDB (b) CBAD (c) BCAD (d) BDAC

4. A. was a cheat
   B. to whom I sold
   C. the man
   D. my house
   (a) BDCA (b) CBDA (c) ACBD (d) CBAD

Directions Q. Nos. 5-8) Place the group of words sequentially to make a suitable sentence.

5. According to ......
   P. make people feel calm or
   Q. to munch on the
   R. Dr Larson, chocolate contains
   S. happy, so next time, if you
   T. about 380 chemicals that
   U. are depressed, don't forget
   .... humble chocolate.
   (a) RUSPQT (b) RTPSUQ
   (c) RPSQTU (d) RTUPQS

6. The company ......
   P. on installing a state of
   Q. second floor of its building
   R. the art gym at the
   S. the employees are not very
   T. spent a lot of money
   U. but it is hardly used; it seems
   .... enthusiastic about it.
   (a) TPRQUS (b) PRTSQU
   (c) USRPTQ (d) RTPUSQ

7. Middle Eastern art ......
   P. painters were often seen in
   Q. was mostly influenced by
   R. exterior walls of mosque
   S. religion as works of great
   T. the doorways, minarets and
   U. religious buildings such as on
   (a) PQRUST (b) PRSQUT
   (c) QSRPTU (d) QSPUTR

8. No, you are ......
   P. a cup of tea, and Do you
   Q. having wrong notions about

R. her I was waiting there

S. call this hospitality?

T. for more than three hours

U. without even being offered

(a) RTUPSQ

(b) STQUVP

(c) QRTUPS

(d) TRPUSQ

9. Rearrange the phrases to make a meaningful sentence.

A. To the problem of

B. comment on whether

C. charity is a solution

D. scarcity or not

Codes

(a) ABCD (b) BCAD (c) CBDA (d) BADC

2 Marks Questions

10. Arrange the sentences suitably.

I loved dancing

P. I graduated, I moved to South Africa

Q. and was retained as an

R. So much but when

S. English teacher, yet I still

Danced professionally in Cape Town

(a) RPQS (b) QSPR (c) PQSR (d) SPRQ

11. Complete this description of a banana leaf by arranging the sentences in proper order.

1. In many restaurants in Kerala, Tamil Nadu and Karnataka, food is served on banana leaves.

2. When the meal is finished, the leaf is disposed off in an environment friendly way.

3. The banana leaf is being used in India for many purposes.

4. Eating food on a banana leaf is considered more hygienic than steel or plastic plates.

(a) 4-1-3-2 (b) 2-4-1-3

(c) 1-4-2-3 (d) 3-1-4-2

12. Put the steps of the recipe in correct sequence.

How to make Pancakes

1. fry the sides nicely and slide those into a plate.

2. pour the batter and when it bubbles turn the pancake.

3. pour some oil in a skillet and set the stove on the heat up.

4. make a batter with flour, eggs, milk and pinch of baking soda.

(a) 1-4-2-3 (b) 4-2-1-3

(c) 4-3-2-1 (d) 4-1-3-2

13. Complete the paragraph by replacing the phrases in bold with their correct order. I moved back to London for my masters. Alongside that, I still teach English, work at a large theatre and also work for a charity group. **Say the most needless of time to** I am exhausted after so much of work.

(a) most of the time, needless to say

(b) needless to say, most of the time

(c) to say the most needless of time

(d) needless of time to say the most

14. Read the sentences and arrange them in a logical order.

A. Delhi is considered one of the greenest cities in the world with twenty per cent of its area covered with forests.

B. That is why Delhi is also fondly called as 'Mini India'. Not only that, but did you know, Delhi has a unique international museum of toilets?

C. It is admired by all the Indians for its rich history and its composite culture.

D. However polluted it may be quoted, Delhi also has a broad green patch in the Ridge Road area, which is known as the 'Lungs of Delhi'.

(a) D-A-B-C (b) A-C-B-D

(c) B-D-C-A (d) A-D-C-B

Fillers

1 Mark Questions

Directions (Q. Nos. 1-5) Read the following passage and select the option that can correctly replace the respective blanks.

Ancient art forms can be found all ...(1)... the world. Some well known ancient art can be ...(2)... in Asian countries like India, China etc. ...(3)... drawings can be seen in the pottery, walls and buildings. Ancient art forms can also be seen in jewelry, sculptures and weapons. In India, various art forms ...(4)... like paintings, architecture, sculpture etc. The rock cut paintings of BhimBetaka and the ...(5)... town planning of Harappa and Mohenjo-Daro are remarkable examples of varied art forms.

1. (a) in   (b) over
    (c) after   (d) through

2. (a) found   (b) retrieved
    (c) originate   (d) set up

3. (a) Attractive
    (b) Exotic
    (c) Popular
    (d) Beautiful

4. (a) produced
    (b) evolved
    (c) fabricated
    (d) manufactured

5. (a) proceeded   (b) progressed
    (c) advanced   (d) complex

Directions (Q. Nos. 6-10) Choose the correct option to fill in the blanks in the given passage.

China also ...(6)... of a rich history of art that shaped up its evolution. Semi precious stones Jade, which ...(7)... from metamorphic rocks were carved into various art forms and jewelry during Neolithic period. Another unique art form was the ...(8)... of graphic art that was put into paper called Calligraphy. It was crafted with ...(9)... and highlighted the understated beauty of Chinese characters. Calligraphy was ...(10)... as a supreme visual art form in ancient China and Japan.

6. (a) brags   (b) tells
    (c) boasts   (d) boast

7. (a) are extracted
    (b) extracted
    (c) is extracted
    (d) were extracted

8. (a) genre
    (b) type
    (c) variety
    (d) All of the above

9. (a) pen and paper
   (b) colour and brush
   (c) brush and ink
   (d) paper and pen

10. (a) viewed
    (b) view
    (c) to be viewed
    (d) viewing

2 Marks Questions

Directions (Q. Nos. 11-20) Replace the words in underline with the correct words to make a meaningful story.

A Scare

It was a ...**(11)** ... <u>hot</u> day of March and it was still cool to sit in the open in the mornings. To enjoy the beauty of the weather, I picked up an interesting book and took my seat on a chair in the garden. There were flowers ...**(12)**... <u>sprinkled in access off</u> with pleasure.

It was an interesting story. I was deeply engrossed over the ...**(13)**... <u>sprinting of the follower</u> to catch his beloved. Suddenly, she tumbled on a stone and fell down. Thud! there was a sound. I suddenly became ...**(14)**... <u>happy and competent</u> of my surroundings. It was not the girl in the story but a big bag that had landed on the lawn just a little distance away from where I was sitting.

I had heard so much about rowdy people ....**(15)**.... <u>mailing bullets</u> that I hurriedly got up from my chair and cried in panic, "Father! Mother!"

They came ...**(16)**... .<u>running out</u>. We looked at the big bag more closely. "Who knows, what is inside? It may be a bomb", we said almost in ...**(17)**... <u>assistance</u>. By then, the neighbours had joined in and ...**(18)**... <u>no one</u> had even dialed No.100. Soon our small garden ...**(19)**... <u>are blocked up with</u> so many people including the people from the bomb squad.

One of them carefully tuned the bag with his stick like instrument that was blinking from one end. O! Someone had thrown a bag full of old used clothes ...**20**... <u>outside their garden</u>.

11. (a) wind   (b) cloudy
    (c) fine   (d) finer

12. (a) peeping all over
    (b) strewn all around
    (c) spread over
    (d) fluttering

13. (a) crossing of the lovers
    (b) glaring of lover
    (c) running of the lover
    (d) dashing lover

14. (a) horrified and scared
    (b) alert and aware
    (c) scared and shouted
    (d) No change

15. (a) shooting bombs
    (b) throwing bombs
    (c) tossing bombs
    (d) Any of the above

16. (a) carefully out   (b) jumping out
    (c) shouting out   (d) No change

17. (a) unison   (b) combination
    (c) agreement   (d) together

18. (a) nobody   (b) someone
    (c) everyone   (d) anyone

19. (a) were full of   (b) is filled of
    (c) was filled with   (d) is fill with

20. (a) in the garden
    (b) in our garden
    (c) into their garden
    (d) No change

Chapter 15

Synonyms and Antonyms

1 Mark Questions

Directions (Q. Nos. 1-7) Select the option which is the synonym of the given word

1. SOLITUDE
   - (a) Musical composition
   - (b) Loneliness
   - (c) Single mindedness
   - (d) True statement

2. VALOUR
   - (a) Wandering
   - (b) Brightness
   - (c) Bravery
   - (d) Affluence

3. TERMINUS
   - (a) Stop
   - (b) Terminal
   - (c) Tenure
   - (d) Junction

4. IMPARTIAL
   - (a) Optimistic
   - (b) Enthusiastic
   - (c) Realistic
   - (d) Unbiased

5. REMORSE
   - (a) Despair
   - (b) Regret
   - (c) Anger
   - (d) Hatred

6. AMICABLE
   - (a) Just
   - (b) Appropriate
   - (c) Durable
   - (d) Friendly

7. DISCREET
   - (a) Well-mannered
   - (b) Mild
   - (c) Proud
   - (d) Prudent

Directions (Q. Nos. 8-14) In the following sentences a word is given in bold. Choose the option nearest in meaning to the word in bold.

8. He gave a **vivid** description of the movie he had seen a week before.
   - (a) Simple
   - (b) Dull
   - (c) Clear
   - (d) Confused

9. **Brevity** is suggested for expressing yourself.
   - (a) Conciseness
   - (b) sharpness
   - (c) intelligence
   - (d) confidence

10. Because of a family **feud**, the whole family was wiped out.
    - (a) Problem
    - (b) Quarrel
    - (c) Crisis
    - (d) Trouble

11. The poet was in **pensive** mood.
    - (a) Sad
    - (b) Thoughtful
    - (c) Gloomy
    - (d) Black

12. The merchant was **renowned** for his simple way of living.
    - (a) Notorious
    - (b) Famous
    - (c) Unknown
    - (d) Notable

13. Since he promised to do so I **presume** he will come.
    - (a) Think
    - (b) Guess
    - (c) Suppose
    - (d) Believe

14. Russia is an enormous country, the largest in the world.
    - (a) Insignificant
    - (b) Obstinate
    - (c) Colossal
    - (d) Populated

15. Find the suitable antonym of the word underlined in the given sentence.

The commission took two years to go through the <u>massive</u> collection of files before publishing a report.

(a) Heavy   (b) Miniscule
(c) Light   (d) Short

16. Find the suitable antonym of the word underlined in the given sentence.
India now produces <u>sufficient</u> quantity of foodgrains every year.

(a) Short   (b) Inadequate
(c) Small   (d) More

17. Select the option that is opposite in meaning to the underlined words.
In ancient days, a <u>fragile</u> glass jar was considered to be more <u>valuable</u> than a human slave.

(a) Broad, Useful   (b) Tall, Important
(c) Strong, Useless (d) Heavy, Priceless

18. Select the antonyms for the underlined words.
One can <u>acquire</u> fame only by being truthful, <u>honest</u> and faithful.

(a) Gain, sincere
(b) Lose, Biased
(c) Win, frank
(d) Attain, direct

19. Choose the word according to the relation of the words given in pair.
Progressive : Regressed :: Varied : ?

(a) Different   (b) Monotonous
(c) Dry   (d) Uniform

20. Find the suitable word according to the relation of the words given in pairs.
Careful : Cautious
Novice : Learner
Boastful: ?

(a) Suspicious   (b) Arrogant
(c) Joyful   (d) Humble

2 Marks Questions

Directions (Q. Nos. 21-23) Some words are given in capital letters and following them a group of synonyms. You have to select the correct group of synonyms for the word.

21. SUPERVISE
A. Divine, hallowed, religious, holy, blessed
B. Agree, concur, fit
C. Manage, administer, oversee, direct, govern
D. None of the above
Codes
(a) Only A   (b) Both B and D
(c) Only C   (d) Only B

22. STRENUOUS
A. Vigorous, hard, difficult, ardvous, energetic.
B. Black, gloomy, solitary, abandoned
C. Wayward, arbitrary, variable
D. None of the above
(a) Both A and B   (b) Only C
(c) Only D   (d) Only A

23. UNANIMOUS
A. Dull, boring, tiresome, hard
B. United, solid, common, universal, unified, undivided
C. Comfortable, capable, able, skilled, qualified, good
D. None of the above
(a) Only B   (b) Both A and C
(c) Both B and D   (d) All of these

Directions (Q. Nos. 24-26) Choose the group of antonyms for the following words.

24. Refurbish
A. Wipe out, Demolish, knock down, Destroy
B. Rehabilitate, Renovate, Renew, Demolish

C. Remodel, Update, Undying, Timeless

D. Virtuous, Destroy, Ruin, Social.

Codes

(a) Only B   (b) Both A and B

(c) Only A   (d) Both C and D

25. Diversity

A. Variety, Medley, Multiplicity, Variation

B. Constancy, Uniformity, Consistency, Conformity

C. Variation, Uniformity, Array, Equality

D. Equity, Sameness, Mixture, Dissimilarity

(a) Only A

(b) Both B and D

(c) Both A and C

(d) Only B

26. Erroneous

A. Flawless, scrupulous, Mistaken, Dicey

B. Wrong, Incorrect, Invalid, Untrue

C. Mistaken, Inaccurate, Correct, Right

D. True, Exact, Unerring, Precise

(a) Only B

(b) Only D

(c) A, B and D

(d) B, C and D

27. Match the words given in List I with their synonyms.

List I	List II
A. Admire	1. Assume
B. Gaiety	2. Happiness
C. Diligent	3. Praise
D. Presume	4. Hardworking

Codes

	A	B	C	D			A	B	C	D
(a)	2	4	1	3		(b)	1	3	2	4
(c)	4	1	3	2		(d)	3	2	4	1

28. Match the words given in List I with their antonyms.

List I	List II
A. Distraught	1. Advance
B. Impede	2. Calm
C. Privilege	3. Coward
D. Gallant	4. Disadvantage

Codes

	A	B	C	D			A	B	C	D
(a)	2	1	4	3		(b)	1	3	2	4
(c)	4	1	3	2		(d)	3	2	4	1

One Word Substitution

1 Mark Questions

Directions (Q. Nos. 1-7) Choose one word for the given sentence.

1. A person who believes in the existence of God
   (a) Theist   (b) Pessimist
   (c) Atheist   (d) Agnostic

2. A kind of disease caused by a micro-organism such as bacteria
   (a) Infection
   (b) Contamination
   (c) Communicable
   (d) Antiseptic

3. A system of government by one person with absolute power
   (a) Aristocracy   (b) Anarchy
   (c) Autocracy   (d) Autonomy

4. A large bedroom for a number of people in a school or institution
   (a) Gymnasium   (b) Dormitory
   (c) Granary   (d) Infirmary

5. A large, tall cupboard for hanging or storing clothes
   (a) Closet   (b) Cabinet
   (c) Almirah   (d) Wardrobe

6. To leave one's native country, region or location
   (a) Immigrate   (b) Emigrate
   (c) Shift   (d) Relocate

7. Killing of one person by another
   (a) Genocide   (b) Suicide
   (c) Homicide   (d) Infanticide

Directions (Q. Nos. 8-12) Choose the correct option for the given professions.

8. A person who composes dance sequences or steps
   (a) Cartographer   (b) Calligrapher
   (c) Choreographer   (d) Chauffeur

9. A person who studies the influence of celestial bodies on human events and the natural world.
   (a) Astronomer   (b) Astrologer
   (c) Space scientist   (d) Geologist

10. A person who practice the art of garden cultivation or management
    (a) Horticulturist   (b) Floriculturist
    (c) Apiculturist   (d) Agriculturist

11. A person who compiles dictionaries
    (a) Lexicographer   (b) Demographer
    (c) Stenographer   (d) Ethnographer

12. A person who describes and maps the surface features of geographic regions
    (a) Cartographer   (b) Topographer
    (c) Bibliographer   (d) Geographer

Directions (Q. Nos. 13-17) Choose the correct option for the given definitions.

13. An extreme or irrational fear of confined or closed places
    - (a) Chronophobia
    - (b) Gynophobia
    - (c) Claustrophobia
    - (d) Cacophobia

14. An extreme or irrational fear of heights
    - (a) Acrophobia
    - (b) Aerophobia
    - (c) Autophobia
    - (d) Ergophobia

15. A collection of historical documents or records providing information about places, people etc
    - (a) Aviary
    - (b) Arena
    - (c) Arsenal
    - (d) Archives

16. A room or a place for the medical treatment of people having chronic illness
    - (a) Planetarium
    - (b) Sanatorium
    - (c) Cloakroom
    - (d) Hospital

17. A branch of study dealing with the behaviour, structure, classification and distribution of animals
    - (a) Zoology
    - (b) Petrology
    - (c) Botany
    - (d) Physiology

Directions (Q. Nos. 18-22) In questions given below, fill in the blanks with the correct alternative.

18. A person who supervises in the examination hall is called a/an ....
    - (a) Checker
    - (b) Investigator
    - (c) Invigilator
    - (d) Examiner

19. Delhi police is keeping track of the kidnapper through electronic ....
    - (a) Survey
    - (b) Surveillance
    - (c) Vigilance
    - (d) Devices

20. There is a lot of .... in the government offices.
    - (a) Bureaucracy
    - (b) Processes
    - (c) Methods
    - (d) Works

21. My brother works as a .... of drawing and paintings at the National Gallery of Modern Art.
    - (a) Guardian
    - (b) Steward
    - (c) Curator
    - (d) Caretaker

22. Life history of a person written by that person is called ....
    - (a) Biography
    - (b) Autobiography
    - (c) Flexography
    - (d) Angiography

2 Marks Questions

23. Choose the correct option for the description of disease.
    Though he has recovered miraculously from that fatal head injury but unfortunately he is facing the condition of ....
    - A. Amnesia
    - B. Insomnia
    - C. Ambrosia
    - D. Forgetfulness
    - (a) Only A
    - (b) Only B
    - (c) Only C
    - (d) Only D

24. Identify the branch of science that deals with the scientific study of mind and behaviour.
    1. Anthropology
    2. Psychology
    3. Philosophy
    4. Phycology
    - (a) Only 1
    - (b) Only 2
    - (c) Both 1 and 2
    - (d) 1, 3 and 4

25. Choose the incorrect option.

A. One who talks of his achievements – Philanthropist

B. A process involving too much official formality- Red-tapism

C. Government wing responsible for making rules –Executive

D. Large number of people affected by a disease-Epidemic

Codes

(a) Only A   (b) Both A and C

(c) Both B and D   (d) Only D

26. Choose the one that can be substituted for the given sentence.

Detailed plan of a journey or a trip to be undertaken

(a) Schedule   (b) Travelogue

(c) Itinerary   (d) Almanac

27. Match the following.

List I	List II
A. Natural plants and vegetation of a place	1. Acquit
B. Constant efforts made to achieve something	2. Flora
C. Trying to settle dispute between two parties	3. Mediator
D. To free a person by verdict of not guilty	4. Perseverance

Codes

	A	B	C	D			A	B	C	D
(a)	2	4	3	1		(b)	4	1	2	3
(c)	3	1	4	2		(d)	2	3	1	4

28. Replace the bold words by the most suitable word to make a proper sentence.

That **self disciplined in order to attain salvation** man, left his big four bedroom apartment and moved into a small hut.

A. Devoted   B. Skeptic

C. Ascetic   D. Poised

(a) Only A

(b) Both B and C

(c) Only C

(d) None of the above

29. Match the following words with their meanings.

List I		List II
A. Ballad	1.	A person who is new to a subject or an activity
B. Archipelago	2.	A poem or song narrating a story in short stanzas
C. Neophyte	3.	Land so surrounded by water as to be almost an island
D. Affidavit	4.	A written statement confirmed by oath or affirmation for use as evidence in court

Codes

	A	B	C	D
(a)	2	4	3	1
(b)	4	1	2	3
(c)	3	1	4	2
(d)	2	3	1	4

Chapter 17

Idioms and Phrases

1 Mark Questions

Directions (Q. Nos. 1-6) Each of the below given idioms is followed by four options. Choose the correct option.

1. To put two and two together
(a) to bear the brunt of
(b) to conclude something
(c) to put on a false appearance
(d) to put off

2. To face the music
(a) to give a music performance
(b) to suffer unpleasant consequences
(c) to suffer hardship
(d) to change things

3. To fight tooth and nail
(a) to fight a losing battle
(b) to fight heroically
(c) to fight in a cowardly manner
(d) to make every possible effort to win

4. Take exception to
(a) different
(b) to take with difficulty
(c) object to
(d) difficult

5. To leave no stone unturned
(a) to keep clean and tidy
(b) to try every possible course of action to achieve something
(c) to work enthusiastically
(d) to change things

6. A hard nut to crack
(a) difficult things require extra effort
(b) a difficult problem to solve
(c) a difficult problem solved easily
(d) costly things need careful handling

Directions (Q. Nos. 7-13) Given below are four alternatives for the idiom underlined in the sentence. Choose the most appropriate option.

7. We <u>kept our fingers crossed</u> till the final results were declared.
(a) kept praying   (b) waited anxiously
(c) felt scared   (d) kept hoping

8. Rajesh scored only forty marks in his English mid-term exam. He needs <u>to pull up his socks</u> to do well in his exams.
(a) to wear better socks
(b) to work hard
(c) to make an effort to improve
(d) to buy good pair of socks

9. Rajiv began to <u>have second thoughts</u> about his decision to study Philosophy when he realised that he could not even pay attention during the lectures.
(a) to think separately
(b) reconsider a decision
(c) to think about others
(d) postpone taking a decision

10. He was unable to <u>account for the deficit</u> in the company's bank balance.
(a) give a satisfactory explanation
(b) speak the truth about
(c) maintain accounts properly
(d) give the accounts

11. The teacher asked the students to <u>break the ice</u> and introduce themselves to each other.
(a) to play together
(b) to work hard
(c) overcome initial shyness
(d) talk to each other

12. The two brothers can never work together. They are always <u>at loggerheads</u>.
(a) fighting with others
(b) playing with each other
(c) differing strongly
(d) to go together

13. I will never bet again. <u>I burnt my fingers</u> betting at the Race Course today.
(a) suffer for doing something stupid
(b) burn finger while cooking
(c) giving money and not getting it back
(d) losing money

Directions (Q. Nos. 14-19) Fill in the blanks in each sentence with the phrasal verbs given in options.

14. He accepted the car .... his claim for 4 lacs.
(a) in accordance with
(b) in lieu of
(c) by way of
(d) on account of

15. .... the light, please. I'd like to get some sleep.
(a) Turn on   (b) Turn round
(c) Turn over   (d) Turn off

16. When you are in town could you .... the books I ordered?
(a) pick up   (b) pick out
(c) pick off   (d) pick over

17. It is written with a pencil so you can .... if you need to.
(a) rub it up   (b) rub it out
(c) rub in   (d) rub along

18. The dog .... and .... trying to catch its tail.
(a) turn over, over
(b) turned round, round
(c) turn off, off
(d) turn on, on

19. We are able to .... much better now that we don't live together.
(a) get on   (b) get in
(c) out   (d) get about

2 Marks Questions

20. Consider the following statements.
1. Since no one came forward to support the movement started by him, he had to **eat humble pie** and give in to the management's demands.
2. The government will have to think twice before applying that policy, for once they **cross the Rubicon**, there is no going back.

Which of these statements show the correct use of the idioms/phrases?
(a) Only 1   (b) Only 2
(c) Both 1 and 2   (d) None of these

21. Choose the sentence that does not show the right use of idioms (in bold).
A. Give me a **ballpark figure** of the cost of renovating this house.

B. In winters the mufflers are **all the rage** but in summers they disappear.

C. Ajit was driving rashly, thank God we returned **all in one piece**.

D. After losing in the game of Chess, Prashant was on **cloud nine** and resigned from it.

Codes

(a) Only A
(b) Both B and C
(c) Both A and D
(d) Only D

22. Complete the second sentence with a phrasal verb so that the meaning of both the sentences are similar.

"Can I <u>rely on</u> you for your support?" said Richa to her husband.

"Can I .... you for your support?" said Richa to her husband.

(a) count on
(b) count in
(c) count up
(d) count with

23. Choose the correct option to complete the sentence that has a phrasal verb and an idiom.

A manager said to his employee, "I personally think you've .... the wrong horse and you've got your .... to the wall.

(a) back, backed
(b) backing, back
(c) backed, back
(d) backed, backing

24. Fill in the blanks with correct idioms/phrases by match the given list.

List I	List II
A. I walked the .... of Amherst street, looking for a chemist.	1. Spic and span
B. I want the drawing room to be .... by the time the guests come.	2. Pros and cons
C. Tell me the .... of taking up this job.	3. Bits and pieces
D. I went shopping, but I didn't buy much, just a few	4. Length and breadth

Codes

	A	B	C	D
(a)	1	4	3	2
(b)	4	1	2	3
(c)	3	1	4	2
(d)	2	3	1	4

25. Match the idioms with their meanings.

List I (Idioms)	List II (Meanings)
A. To get through	1. To reach the same standard or position
B. To catch up	2. To start on working something
C. To fall behind	3. To pass an exam or a test
D. To get down to	4. To be behind in a task

Codes

	A	B	C	D
(a)	1	4	3	2
(b)	4	1	2	3
(c)	3	1	4	2
(d)	2	3	1	4

Reading Comprehension

1 Mark Questions

Directions (Q. Nos. 1-5) Read the passage given below and answer the questions that follow by selecting the correct option.

The Great Barrier Reef

Where are the most biologically diverse places on the planet? If I asked you this question, you might guess the Amazon rainforest in Brazil or the jungles of India. But another rich source of **biodiversity** is actually underwater. Off the North Eastern coast of Australia live thousands of species of fish, birds and reptiles. Their home is the Great Barrier Reef, the world's largest coral reef. Stretching over 1600 miles, the Great Barrier Reef is as long as the distance from Boston to Miami in the United States. It covers more than 133000 square miles and it is even visible from outer space. Scientists believe that the reef is around 500000 years old, but it has shifted forms several times during its existence. The reef has most likely had its present topology for 6000-8000 years.

The reef may look like a rock, but it's actually alive. Coral reefs are underwater structures that are made by corals — tiny animals that are related to jellyfish. The corals have tender bodies that are vulnerable to attack, so they secrete a hard substance called calcium carbonate to protect their exteriors. The calcium carbonate builds up until it makes formations that look like rocks to the human eye. Coral reefs grow best in warm, shallow, clear water that receives a lot of sunshine. Around a quarter of all marine species live in coral reefs and these reefs play an important role in supporting diversity in the ocean. Charles Darwin, the famous biologist who first proposed the scientific theory of evolution, described the coral reef as an oasis in the desert of the ocean. Though tropical waters typically provide very little nutrients, the coral reefs that exist in tropical waters are among the richest and most diverse ecosystems on Earth.

Hundreds of different coral species make up the various structures composing the Great Barrier Reef. Within these structures, several ecosystems **flourish**. Ecosystems are complex systems that contain several species that interact with one another. The Great Barrier Reef is home to over 1500 species of fish. But it's not just fish that live in the reef. The reef also provides food and shelter to sponges, whales, dolphins, marine turtles and molluscs.

1. The Great Barrier Reef is
   (a) a mammal that comes to the ocean's surface to breathe every 7 to 15 minutes.
   (b) something that is made out of the same material as human fingernails.

    (c) the world's largest coral reef located off the North Eastern coast of Australia.

    (d) a large part of the Amazon rainforest located in the country of Brazil.

2. What are coral reefs?

    (a) coral reefs are underwater structures.

    (b) coral reefs are rocks of calcium.

    (c) coral reefs are small jellyfish type of small animals.

    (d) a combination of different types of reefs.

3. The word in the third line of the first paragraph 'biodiversity' means

    (a) multifariousness.

    (b) similarity.

    (c) a variety of different types of plant and animal life.

    (d) identical.

4. The antonym of flourish (para 3) is

    (a) ornamentation

    (b) thrive

    (b) accomplishment

    (d) flounder

5. The Barrier Reef is a food provider to

    (a) sponges

    (b) whales

    (c) dolphins and turtles

    (d) All of the above

Directions (Q. Nos. 6-10) Read the following poem and answer the questions by selecting the correct option.

Moonlight

Deep in the night
When all is still
A moon beam climbs the window-sill
Over your bed
It softly flies
To see if sleep has closed your eyes
A pinch of gold
Some fairy sand
It clasped within that moonbeam's hand
And if by chance
You're not asleep
It comes tip-toe on gentle feet
To touch your eyes
With golden beams
And take you to the land of dreams

6. The Poet speaks of the moonlight as if it were a ....

    (a) watchman   (b) thief

    (c) shadow   (d) fairy

7. The poet has used the expression to describe 'A pinch of gold' and 'Some fairy sand' as ....

    (a) Child's dream world

    (b) Colour of the moon

    (c) Face of an innocent child

    (d) Face of the moon

8. A soothing effect of the moonlight is ....

    (a) It puts child to sleep

    (b) It rubs a pinch of golden sand

    (c) It climbs the window-sill

    (d) It tip-toes on the gentle feet

9. The 'you' in the poem most probably is ....

    (a) The poet

    (b) A mother

    (c) A little child

    (d) A golden fairy

10. Which among the following lines describes the silent movement of the moon light?

    (a) Deep in the night

    (b) Everything is still

    (c) Comes tip-toe on gentle feet

    (d) Climbs the window-sill

2 Marks Questions

Directions (Q. Nos. 11-20) Read the passage given below and answer the questions that follow by selecting the correct option.

When I was a child, my father always read to me before my bedtime. My favourite author was and still is Enid Blyton, one of the most famous story writers in history. She had written hundreds of interesting books that have **enthralled** millions of children around the world through the years. These have even been translated into dozens of languages and have remained one of the best selling and most popular publications of all time.

Enid Blyton's stories are always very exciting and imaginative. Her detective stories usually have a few children coming together to solve mysteries. I love seeing these young detectives triumphing over evil villains and criminals. Also, these children are just like ourselves. They have homework to do and school to attend. Their bravery and determination to solve mysteries and help the weak and the oppressed is admirable and holds a very valuable lesson for all of us.

As for her fantasy stories, Enid Blyton has created a whole new magical world out of her imagination. In this world, forests come alive at night with elves, goblins and talking animals. A climb to the top of some trees would often lead to the discovery of whole new lands. Every tunnel can lead to treasures and every hole in the ground is an adventure waiting for courageous children with wits and bravery. A rainbow always leads to a pot of gold.

My favourite character is Old Mr Saucepan. He lives in the trunk of the magical Faraway Tree. With his body covered all over with utensils, which he wears instead of a normal shirt, Mr Saucepan often leads the children into one adventure after another.

Many times he can be caught falling asleep at the most critical moments and has to be rescued by the children repeatedly. At other times, when the children are in danger, he would leap in and fight away any nasty creatures which are threatening them. **Clumsy** but lovable, his concern for the children, whom he adores, is really touching.

I will never grow too old to read these books and their magic will always live in my heart. I hope that someday I too may pass them on to my children so that together we can escape into this wonderful magical world of stories.

11. The writer says that she enjoys reading Enid Blyton's stories because
    (a) millions of children around the world have read these stories
    (b) her books are always very exciting and imaginative
    (c) there are children in the stories solving mysteries
    (d) she is one of the most famous story writers in history.

12. Enid Blyton's books are read by children in many countries throughout the world because ....
    (a) her stories always have good endings
    (b) there are elves, goblins and talking animals
    (c) her stories involve young children solving mysteries
    (d) her books have been translated into many different languages

13. The 'Fantasy stories' refers to stories of ....

   (a) detective adventures

   (b) Mr Saucepan rescuing children whom he adores

   (c) climbing on top of trees

   (d) magic and imagination

14. The word 'enthralled' (para 1) means ....

   (a) to put on hold

   (b) captivate

   (c) wonderful

   (d) delightful

15. Which of the following is not a synonym of clumsy (Para 4)?

   (a) awkward   (b) graceful

   (c) inept   (d) ungainly

Directions (Q. Nos. 16-20) Read the following poem and answer the question that follow by selecting the correct option.

Indian Weavers

Weavers, weaving at break of day,
Why do you weave a garment so gay?
Blue as the wing of a bluebird wild,
We weave the robes of a new-born child.
Weavers, weaving at fall of night,
Why do you weave a garment so bright?
Like the plumes of a peacock, purple and green,
We weave the marriage-veils of a queen.
Weavers, weaving solemn and still,

What do you weave in the moonlight chill?
White as a feather and white as a cloud,
We weave a dead man's funeral shroud.

16. Whom does the poet address in the poem?

   (a) Infants   (b) Queens

   (c) Weavers   (b) All of these

17. What do the weavers weave in the early morning time?

   (a) A dull grey cloth

   (b) A soft white cloth

   (c) Purple and green cloth

   (d) A bright blue cloth

18. What do the weavers weave in the chilly moonlight?

   (a) A garment light as a feather

   (b) A garment to keep the chill wind away

   (c) A garment meant to cover a dead man

   (d) A garment to wrap a newborn child

19. The three stages of life mentioned in the poem are ....

   (a) infancy, childhood and old age

   (b) infancy, youth and death

   (c) infancy, adolescence, middle age

   (d) childhood, adulthood, senility

20. What do the weavers weave at the fall of night?

   (a) A blue robe

   (b) A white shroud

   (c) A marriage-veil for the queen

   (d) I garment like a feather

Writing Skills

1 Mark Questions

Directions (Q. Nos. 1-8) You are Smita living in the hostel of ABC school, New Delhi. Fill in the banks to complete the letter to your sister Rani describing your hostel life. Choose from the given options.

Sameera Hostel
ABC School
New Delhi
6th December 20XX

My dear Rani,

I received your loving letter three days ago, but because of my pre-occupation in making preparations for the annual function of our hostel, ...(1)..... .

I feel pleased in informing you that ....(2).... in the General Knowledge Quiz and our team stood second in the folk dance competition ....(3).... . As I am staying in the hostel, I ....(4).... more than two hours daily in improving my general knowledge and current affairs in addition to course studies.

Ours is a good hostel. Most of the students are .....(5)..... . Our hostel warden is a very strict lady. She keeps a ....(6)...... on all our activities. The quality of food being served is quite good, consisting of nutritious cereals and vegetables. Breakfast and other meals .....(7)..... at a fixed time and we have to be there not to miss them. In the evening we play games like badminton and tennis. As such, I find this hostel as .....(8)..... with everything of good quality.

What about you? How are your studies going on ? Do write to me for any help or work.

Convey my regards to Mom and Daddy. Yours affectionately.

Smita

1. (a) I could not write to you
   (b) I could not spare time to reply you
   (c) I couldn't get time at all
   (d) I could not answer you

2. (a) I was appreciated
   (b) I stood first
   (c) I secured praise
   (d) I achieved

3. (a) held during the annual function programmes
   (b) organised annual function
   (c) displayed during Annual Day
   (d) held on the Annual Day

4. (a) am giving   (b) am spending
   (c) am devoting   (d) am sparing

5. (a) well disciplined   (b) well behaved
   (c) well cared of   (d) well managed

6. (a) strict eye   (b) close eye
   (c) close watch   (d) vigilance

7. (a) are served   (b) are being served
    (c) is served   (d) get serve

8. (a) beautifully done up
    (b) well prepared
    (c) well-maintained
    (d) well looked after

Directions (Q. Nos. 9-13) You are Group Leader, N S S Camp of DAV Public School, Daryaganj, New Delhi. Fill in the blanks to complete the notice given below. Choose from the given options.

9
10

20th December, 20XX

NSS Camp

All the students are informed that a NSS camp will be held from 2nd January 20XX to 8th January 20XX in Ghitorni Boys Sr. Secondary School near Mehrauli. Projects include Health [11] and Cleanliness [12]. Volunteers [13] to the undersigned by 25th December 2014.

Mansi
Group Leader

---

9. (a) Notice   (b) Appeal
    (c) NSS Camp   (d) Cleanliness Drive

10. (a) Notice
    (b) Group Leader
    (c) DAV Public School, Daryaganj
    (d) Health Drive

11. (a) illnesses   (b) improvement
    (c) projects   (d) drives

12. (a) Campaigning   (b) Drive
    (c) Schedule   (d) Time table

13. (a) may state their names
    (b) should take notice of
    (c) must give their names
    (d) do give their names

Directions (Q. Nos. 14-21) Read the following essay and fill in the blanks.

Einstein : the Genius

Einstein is the man who …**(14)**… recognises, even if they don't understand his theories, In fact, Einstein is usually referred to as 'Einstein — the genius'. With such a build-up, it isn't surprising that …**(15)**… should feel intimidated at the thought of reading, let alone understanding, Einstein's work.

But Einstein was as human as all of us and had several …**(16)**… . He made no bones about the fact that he was not very good at Mathematics. In fact, …**(17)**… on his part was responsible for his not noticing that the universe was expanding. He had, by oversight, divided a large number by zero and failed to realise this fact! For this reason, he usually had a mathematician with him, whose job was to …**(18)**… the problems Einstein put before him and check their validity.

What was Albert Einstein's contribution to the world of Science? The first of these was the Theory of Relativity. According to Einstein, …**(19)**… is fixed. Both of these are relative to the observer and to the thing being observed. Einstein's second most important contribution was the mass-energy equivalence formula that he …**(20)**… . Energy, according to Einstein, was equivalent to mass multiplied by the speed of light squared. But in Einstein's own opinion his greatest idea after the theory of relativity was to add an egg ...**(21)**... soup. How would this help the world of Science? It would not, but it would help him get a soft-boiled egg to eat, without the trouble caused by having an extra pot to wash!

14. (a) none   (b) everyone
    (c) someone   (d) anyone

15. (a) most of us   (b) all of us
    (c) most of you   (d) none of us

16. (a) ifs and buts
    (b) pros and cons
    (c) faults and weaknesses
    (d) None of the above

17. (a) an intellegent mistake
    (b) a clever mistake
    (c) an important fault
    (d) a silly mistake

18. (a) rectify   (b) examine
    (c) write   (d) read

19. (a) either space or time
    (b) neither space or time
    (c) neither space nor time
    (d) either space nor time

20. (a) develop   (b) developing
    (c) developed   (d) will develop

21. (a) after eating   (b) with cooking
    (c) in cooking   (d) while cooking

2 Marks Questions

22. Fill in the blank.
Formal letters cannot be written in the form of ....

(a) Complaint letters   (b) Application
(c) Resignation letter (d) Friendly letters

Directions (Q. Nos. 23-26) Given below is a letter of complaint with some blanks which are numbered. Fill in the blanks in an appropriate manner so that the letter is completed meaningfully and select the correct option accordingly.

25, Rajouri Garden
New Delhi - 110065
8th December 20XX
The Circulation Manager
Outlook Magazine
A B 10, S J Enclave
New Delhi–110029

Subject : Non-Receipt of Gift

Dear Sir/Madam

I am writing this letter in .....**(23)**...... you advertised about for OUTLOOK magazine in your issue dated 6th November 20XX. I had sent the subscription .....**(24)**...... (Cheque No. 270185 dated 6th November 20XX) for a three year subscription. I received .....**(25)**...... on 1st December 20XX. Unfortunately I have not received .....**(26)**...... Please send the gift as soon as possible. I hope it will not be necessary to remind you again.

Yours truly,

Geeta Vaidya

23. (a) concentration with the special subscription
    (b) connection with the special subscription
    (c) confidence with the special subscription
    (d) concern with the special subscription

24. (a) form along with a cheque of ₹ 1300/-
    (b) document with a cheque of ₹ 1300/-
    (c) structure including a cheque of ₹ 1300/-
    (d) file besides a cheque of ₹ 1300/-

25. (a) all the issues of OUTLOOK
(b) not even a single issue of OUTLOOK
(c) the first issue of OUTLOOK
(d) None of the above

26. (a) the order said by you
(b) the gift promised by you
(c) something which is due from you
(d) Any of the above

Directions (Q. Nos. 27-30) Fill in the blanks to complete the paragraph.

Over the booming loudspeakers, the names of all the …**(27)**… for the next event were called. Dhyuti, had been preparing …**(28)**… for this event all year. She knew her prospects of winning the race were high. Even so, as she stood at the starting point, she felt …**(29)**… . Looking around her at the cheering supporters however her momentary hesitation …**(30)**… .

27. (a) participants   (b) competitors
(c) opposition   (d) people

28. (a) diligently   (b) painfully
(c) hardly   (d) wisely

29. (a) nauseating   (b) ill
(c) nervous   (d) unbalanced

30. (a) shattered   (b) intensified
(c) disappeared   (d) escaped

Directions (Q. Nos. 31 and 32) This is a Diary Entry written by Anita. Read the following and fill in the blanks.

21st November, 2020
Saturday, 10:30 PM
Dear …..**(31)**…… ,

Today, I am going to tell you about an unusual fruit that was brought by Uncle Levin. The fruit is attractively colored. It's outer covering was red and it looked like a bulging rose bud. The inside is soft milky white flesh speckled with tiny black seeds. Uncle said that it is called Dragon fruit and was imported from Vietnam.

I ate a small piece and liked its flavor. I will ask mother to buy it in larger quantities. Uncle told us that the fruit is considered the symbol of luck and good fortune.

Now, I am feeling sleepy, must retire to my bed.

……**(32)**…..

31. (a) Anita
(b) uncle
(c) mother
(d) diary

32. (a) Best wishes
(b) Yours affectionately
(c) Good night
(d) Take care

Chapter 20

Communication Skills

1 Mark Questions

Directions (Q. Nos. 1-7) Select the correct option that defines the following sentence.

1. All the students are appealed not to touch any of the exhibits while visiting this museum.
   - (a) Fact
   - (b) Request
   - (c) Threat
   - (d) Opinion

2. People should not be allowed to use their cell phones in an auditorium.
   - (a) Opinion
   - (b) Order
   - (c) Fact
   - (d) Can't say

3. Vigorous exercises make you sweat and help in eliminating toxins.
   - (a) Threat
   - (b) Fact
   - (c) Opinion
   - (d) Can't say

4. "Open your books on page no. 78, chapter no. 12", said the teacher.
   - (a) Opinion
   - (b) Fact
   - (c) Request
   - (d) Order

5. If you tell someone, you will face dire consequences.
   - (a) Order
   - (b) Threat
   - (c) Fact
   - (d) Opinion

6. Smoke detectors can help save us from fire accidents.
   - (a) Opinion
   - (b) Fact
   - (c) Can't say
   - (d) None of the above

7. Keep smiling, even if you feel terribly disgusted.
   - (a) Fact
   - (b) Request
   - (c) Opinion
   - (d) Both (b) and (c)

Directions (Q. Nos. 8-12) Read the following statements and choose the correct option from the given alternatives.

8. Your friend has not invited you to his birthday party. How will you ....?
   - (a) hold grudge against him
   - (b) send him birthday wishes
   - (c) attend the party somehow
   - (d) ignore the whole situation

9. You are interviewed for a job. At that time, which of the following is most important for you?
   - (a) Opportunities for promotion.
   - (b) Check the remuneration and other facilities.
   - (c) Scope of improvement of skill set.
   - (d) All of the above

10. While you board a bus for a long journey, you notice an unclaimed bag lying on the overhead rack of your seat, you would
    - (a) Ignore it as it do not belongs to you.
    - (b) Open the bag to see if it contains something harmful.
    - (c) Report to the bus driver or conductor
    - (d) Finding no one to claim it, you take it.

11. During the Maths examination, you found that you have not brought your Geometry box. What is the best thing you would do?

    (a) Tell the examiner and ask if it can be arranged.

    (b) Not attempt the geometry questions.

    (c) Ask from students sitting around you.

    (d) Attempt questions without geometry tools.

12. You are living in a hostel and you notice that the food served is of sub standard quality. What would be the best step?

    (a) Leave eating that food and prepare your own food.

    (b) Speak to the cook about it.

    (c) Bring the matter to the hostel in-charge.

    (d) Hire a separate tiffin service for yourself.

Directions (Q. Nos. 13-20) Select the appropriate option to fill in the blanks in the telephonic conversation between Mohit and Nia.

Mohit Hello, can I speak to Nikhil?

Nia Nikhil is not at home right now. ....(13)....

Mohit This is mohit, his friend. ....(14)....

Nia ....(15)...., his sister.

Mohit Hello Nia, ...(16)....

Nia Nikhil ....(17).... to attend his swimming classes.

Mohit ok, ...(18).....

Nia ....(19).... .

Mohit We have a special class tomorrow morning so ....(20)....

Nia I will. Anything else?

Mohit No, Thank you bye

Nia Bye

13. (a) Who are you?
    (b) Who is there?
    (c) Who is speaking?
    (d) Who is saying?

14. (a) May I know who is on the line?
    (b) Would you tell me, who are you?
    (c) Could I know who is on the line?
    (d) Please care to tell me who is there?

15. (a) It is Nia   (b) She is Nia
    (c) This is Nia   (d) Any of these

16. (a) What is Nikhil doing?
    (b) Why Nikhil is not on the line
    (c) Where is Nikhil?
    (d) Where has Nikhil gone?

17. (a) has gone out
    (b) had gone out
    (c) have gone out
    (d) was gone out

18. (a) give a message to Nikhil.
    (b) give him a message, will you?
    (c) can you please give him a message?
    (d) note down the message and tell him.

19. (a) Ok, tell me   (b) Certainly
    (c) Sure, tell me   (d) Any of these

20. (a) therefore he might reach school early tomorrow.
    (b) ask him to reach school early tomorrow.
    (c) so can he reach school early tomorrow?
    (d) in order to that he may reach school early tomorrow.

2 Marks Questions

21. Choose the option that is the correct transformation of the given sentence without changing its meaning.

I only take my lunch in college if I am staying back for extra classes.

(a) When I am not taking my lunch then I do not stay for extra classes in my college.

(b) If I am staying back for extra classes in my college then I do not take my lunch.

(c) I do not take my lunch in college unless I am staying back for extra classes.

(d) I am staying back for extra classes in my college as well as for my lunch.

22. Read the dialogue and complete the conversation.

Doctor Take this syrup for two weeks and you will start to feel better.

Patient..........................

Doctor Are you sure? This is the best medicine for your illness.

Patient Yes, I am sure.

(a) This syrup may cause side effects, isn't it?

(b) I don't need it right now, may be later.

(c) Tell me the doses that needs to be taken

(d) I've had it before and it did not help me.

23. Without changing the meaning of the given sentence, choose the option that best transforms it.

He managed to send his children to foreign university although he was poor.

(a) Though he was poor, he sustained to send his children to foreign universities.

(b) Inspite of living in poverty, he did succeeded to secure foreign university for his children.

(c) Despite him sending his children to foreign university he still lived in poverty.

(d) Even though he made efforts to send his children to foreign university, he could not get success.

24. Situation-Reaction test

During a train journey, at mid night you wake up by a certain sound. You found that someone is trying to steal from the window. You would—

(a) Pull the chain immediately

(b) Raise the alarm

(c) Call the police

(d) Pretend to sleep

25. Fill in the blanks to complete the conversation given below.

Receptionist Sir, if you want a hotel room with the view of the open sea, then it will be ....

Client Sure, please book it for me.

Receptionist Alright, can I have your ID please?

Client .... it is.

(a) cheaper, where   (b) costly, there

(c) cheap, that   (d) costlier, here

26. In this question two statements are given. Find out which of these sentence is a fact and which is an opinion. Mark F for fact and O for opinion.

1. Thunderstorms are very frightening.

2. There is more number of thunderstorms in summers than in winters.

(a) 1-F, 2-O   (b) 1-O, 2-F

(c) 1-F, 2-F   (d) 1-O, 2-O

PRACTICE SET 01

1 Mark Questions

Directions (Q. Nos. 1-5) Read the passage carefully and select the option that you consider the most appropriate answer to each question.

Computers have become so necessary to modern living that it is difficult to believe that they are a relatively recent invention. Undoubtedly, they have proved to be of great value, but they also have their disadvantages. For one thing, they have added to our already large number of crimes.

Hacking was the first computer crime that most of us became aware of. By using their computing expertise, people known as hackers can gain unauthorised access to someone else's computer and make use of the data which they find there. They may, for example, get hold of lists of the names of their competitors' clients and use these to build up their own business or they may use hacking as a form of industrial espionage to find out a rival company's plans. Other hacking activities may be more obviously criminal, in that hackers may log on to financial data in someone else's computer and either alter it illegally or use it for fraudulent purposes.

The possibility of serious financial fraud has been greatly increased by the modern practice of purchasing goods through the Internet. Apparently, the use of credit cards to pay for such purchases has led to record levels of fraud with a great many people being swindled out of a great deal of money. Banks are working hard to improve online security and to provide safeguards for customers, but fraudsters are working just as hard to improve their crooked techniques.

Many computer users worry in case their systems are affected by computer viruses. The people who introduce such bugs into other people's computer programs may not intentionally be committing a crime, but may be doing so as an act of mischief or spite. The motive does not really matter to the people whose data has been deleted or altered or whose files have been corrupted.

Computers are part of a highly technical method of working, in which there are constantly new developments. Unfortunately, there is also a constant stream of new developments in the fraud industry associated with them. All computer users must be on their guard.

1. Unauthorised access to someone else's computer is called ....
   (a) Spying   (b) Interpretation
   (c) Hacking   (d) Virus entry

2. Computer files can be damaged by mischief makers using ....
   (a) innovative methods
   (b) corrupted files
   (c) computer programmes
   (d) computer virus

3. What is required on the part of a computer user? He should be ....
   (a) well-informed
   (b) not using the computer
   (c) aware of corrupt practices
   (d) doing no online shopping

4. The idiom 'on their guard' means ....
   (a) to ignore
   (b) watching out for signs of danger or difficulty
   (c) guarding themselves
   (d) alert against being robbed

5. The word 'swindle' means ....
   (a) a fradulent scheme or option
   (b) use deception to deprive someone out of money
   (c) to sway or move (d) to help

Directions (Q. Nos. 6 and 7) Fill in the blanks using correct tense of the verb given in brackets immediately after the blank and accordingly select the best option.

6. She........ (annoyed, be) with me because I was late and she ....(wait) for a long time.
   (a) is annoyed, is waiting
   (b) was annoyed, had been waiting
   (c) was annoyed, has been waiting
   (d) will be annoyed, is waiting

7. Manish ....(give up) smoking one year ago after a heart attack. He ....(smoked) for thirty years but he gave it up in one go.
   (a) gives up, has been smoking
   (b) gave up, had been smoking
   (c) has given up, has smoked
   (d) gave up, had smoked

Directions (Q. Nos. 8 and 9) Find the antonym of the word underlined by choosing the correct option.

8. Let us not <u>aggravate</u> the sufferings of the poor.
   (a) Abbreviate   (b) Alleviate
   (c) Advocate   (d) Appreciate

9. <u>Miscellaneous</u> items were discussed at the meeting.
   (a) Minor   (b) Unrelated
   (c) Mixed   (d) Homogeneous

Directions (Q. Nos. 10 and 11) Choose the synonym of the underlined words in the sentences.

10. The operator was praised for his <u>dexterity</u>.
    (a) Co-operation   (b) Courtesy
    (c) Punctuality   (d) Skill

11. We did not believe in his statement, but <u>subsequent</u> events proved that he was right.
    (a) Earlier (b) Many (c) Later   (d) Few

Directions (Q. Nos. 12 and 13) Change the following sentence into passive voice so that it expresses the same idea and accordingly choose the correct option.

12. A stone struck me on the head.
    (a) I was struck on a stone by the head.
    (b) I had been struck by a stone on the head.
    (c) I was struck on the head by a stone.
    (d) My head was struck by a stone.

13. The French surrendered Quebec to the English in 1759.
    (a) Quebec was surrendered by the French to the English in 1759.
    (b) Quebec was surrendered to the English in 1759 by the French.
    (c) The English were surrendered Quebec in 1759 by the French.
    (d) Quebec was surrendered in 1759 by the French to the English.

Directions (Q. Nos. 14 and 15) Change the sentence into reported speech. Choose the correct option.

14. The traveller said, "Can you tell me the way to the nearest hotel?" "Yes", said the guard.
    (a) The traveller said to the guard if he can tell him the way to the nearest hotel. The guard replied yes he could.
    (b) The traveller asked the guard if he could tell him the way to the nearest hotel. The guard replied that he could.
    (c) The traveller told the guard to tell him the way to the nearest hotel the guard replied that yes he could.
    (d) The traveller enquired the guard if he knows the way to the nearest hotel. The guard replied that yes he knows the way.

15. My friend said to me, "Has your father returned from the Canada trip?"
    (a) My friend told me if my father has returned from Canada trip?
    (b) My friend asked me if my father had returned from the Canada trip.
    (c) My friend told me that his father had returned from Canada trip.
    (d) My friend enquired me if his father had returned from Canada trip.

Directions (Q. Nos. 16-18) Fill in the blanks with suitable articles or determiners and accordingly select the best option.

16. Last night .... moon was shining brightly. We five friends decided to go for .... moonlight picnic.
    (a) a, an
    (b) a, the
    (c) the,a
    (d) the, the

17. I have known my husband, since I was 10. We lived in .... same street when we were children. Shyam had .... older brother Kartik; I thought he was .... most handsome boy in the world.
    (a) the, an, the
    (b) an, a, the
    (c) the, a, an
    (d) the, the, an

18. He has been sent to prison .... times but has not shown .... sign of improvement.
    (a) many, a
    (b) several, some
    (c) several, any
    (d) many, a

19. Fill in the blank with the most suitable connector and select the option accordingly. Manisha said that she didn't mind where we went .... she didn't have to do any cooking.
    (a) if
    (b) unless
    (c) as long as
    (d) but

Direction (Q. No. 20) Select the option nearest to the meaning of the idiom underlined in the given sentence.

20. This place affords a <u>bird's eye view</u> of the green valley below.
    (a) Beautiful view
    (b) Narrow view
    (c) Limited view
    (d) Aerial view

21. Choose the meaning of the given proverb. Empty bags cannot stand upright.
    (a) Every bad or negative can yield some positives.
    (b) A poor and hungry cannot discharge his duties well.
    (c) Even the unluckiest of unfortunate will taste success sometime.
    (d) Be resilient and try desperate failures, that's how to succeed.

Direction (Q. No. 22) Punctuate the given sentence to make it meaningful and accordingly select the best option.

22. Spencer the great english poet lived in the time of queen Elizabeth
    (a) Spencer, the great English poet lived in the time of queen Elizabeth.
    (b) Spencer, the great English poet, lived in the time of Queen Elizabeth.
    (c) Specer the great English poet; lived in the time of queen Elizabeth.
    (d) Spencer; the great English poet, lived in the time of queen Elizabeth.

Directions (Q. Nos. 23 and 24) Fill in the blanks with the most appropriate form of verb and choose the correct option accordingly.

23. He promised me that he........pay my fee but he didn't. Now I ....pay a fine.
    (a) will, must
    (b) would, should
    (c) would, have to
    (d) would, had to

24. "I haven't seen Rakesh." "Well, he .... studying or playing. He ....go anywhere else."
    (a) may, need not
    (b) must, cannot
    (c) might be, dare not
    (d) might be, should

Direction (Q. No. 25) Fill in the blank with an appropriate preposition. Choose from the options.

25. The headdress of the Cossacks is similar .... that of the ancient Persians.
    (a) in
    (b) to
    (c) with
    (d) at

Directions (Q. No. 26 and 27) Fill in the blanks with the most appropriate form of verb and accordingly choose the best option.

26. You .... him that gambling would ruin him if he didn't put a stop to it.
    (a) should tell
    (b) should warn
    (c) should have warned
    (d) must warn

27. My brother cautioned me and said that
I .... to Delhi in this bitter cold.
(a) should not go
(b) dare not go
(c) need not to have gone
(d) need not go

Directions (Q. Nos. 28-30) Find the option which is different from the others in any respect from the four options given.

28. (a) Inch (b) Foot
(c) Quart (d) Yard

29. (a) Sleet (b) Fog
(c) Vapour (d) Hail stone

30. (a) Illustrious (b) Horrid
(c) Sublime (d) Acclaimed

Directions (Q. Nos. 31-33) In the sentences below, the first and last parts are identified as A and Z. The remaining four are labelled as P, Q, R and S. Find the correct sequence of these four parts and select the correct option accordingly.

31. A : I wasn't sure
P : to hear his voice
Q : in my heart of hearts
R : through that window once more
S : that I really wished
Z : or never to see him there again.
(a) Q P R S (b) S Q P R
(c) P R S Q (d) R S Q P

32. A : Ashoka was successful
P : by the cruelty and horrors of war
Q : he was so disgusted
R : in his military operations
S : and was alone among conquerors
Z : that he renounced it
(a) R S Q P (b) P S Q R
(c) S Q P R (d) Q P R S

33. A : Gold is bright yellow
P : the most Q : in colour
R : beautiful of S : and it is
Z : all the metals
(a) Q S P R (b) S P Q R
(c) S Q R P (d) Q P R S

Directions (Q. Nos. 34-39) A notice is given below with some parts missing but substituted with rectangles with numbers 34 to 39. Identify the text from the given options so that the numbers can be substituted correctly.

> **Sardar Vallabhbhai Patel School, Ahmedabad**
>
> **34**
>
> **25th December, 20XX**
>
> **Science Fair**
>
> Attention Students!
>
> **35** of World Science Day, India Meteorological Department **36** a science fair in our school grounds from 2nd January to 5th January 20XX. The **37** of the fair will be from 9 am to 4 pm. The **38** ₹ 15 per student. You **39** in the model making competition being organised on the occasion. Don't miss this golden opportunity.
>
> Prafull Mishra
>
> Head Boy
>
> XII C.

34. (a) Appeal (b) Notification
(c) A report (d) Notice

35. (a) Because of
(b) On behalf of
(c) On the occasion of
(d) On the situation

36. (a) Will organising
(b) is organising
(c) is going to organise
(d) Both (a) and (c)

37. (a) timings of
(b) occasion of
(c) entry
(d) None of the above

38. (a) exhibition fee will be
(b) fair fee will be
(c) entry fee will be
(d) school fee will be

39. (a) participate
(b) can also participate
(c) might also participate
(d) might participate

Direction (Q. No. 40) Punctuate the given sentence to make it meaningful. Accordingly select the best option.

40. alas what a fool i am he has after all cheated me.
 (a) Alas! What a fool I am! He has, after all, cheated me.
 (b) Alas! What a fool I am? he has, after all cheated me.
 (c) alas! What a fool, I am? He has, after all, cheated me.
 (d) Alas! What a fool I am? he has after; all cheated me.

2 Marks Questions

Direction (Q. No. 41) Fill in the blanks using correct tense of the verb given in the brackets immediately after the blank and accordingly select the best option.

41. He .... (leave) New Delhi last month. Now he lives in Mumbai where he .... (start) his import/export business.
 (a) left, started   (b) has left, has started
 (c) left, has started   (d) left, had started

Direction (Q. No. 42) Fill in the blanks with correct articles.

42. .... Rajputs belong to .... martial race because they were organised into .... force to fight against .... oppression of the rulers.
 (a) The, a, the, the   (b) The, a, a, the
 (c) The, a, an, the   (d) The, a, a, an

Direction (Q. No. 43) Fill in the blanks with the most suitable connectors and accordingly select the best option.

43. The boys encountered lots of problems .... trying to get to the island. ...., they managed to reach the island in time before the sharks came.
 (a) when, But   (b) during, However
 (c) while, Nevertheless
 (d) as, However

44. Select the option nearest to the meaning of the idiom underlined in the given sentence. He is always <u>picking holes in</u> every project.
 (a) asking irrelevant questions on
 (b) suggesting improvements
 (c) finding fault with
 (d) creating problems in

Direction (Q. No. 45) In the passage below, the first and last sentences are identified as A and Z. The remaining four sentences are labelled as P, Q, R, S. Find the correct sequence of these four sentences and select the correct option.

45. A : On vacation in Morocco my friend and I sat down at a street cafe.
 P : At one point he bent over with a big smile, showing a gold tooth.
 Q : Soon I felt the presence of someone standing alongside me.
 R : But this one wouldn't budge.
 S : We had been cautioned about beggars and were told to ignore them. So we did.
 Z : Finally a man walked over to me and whispered, "Hey buddy, this guy's your waiter and he wants your order."

The proper sequence should be
 (a) S Q P R   (b) S Q R P
 (c) Q S R P   (d) Q S P R

46. Match the following.

	List-I		List-II
A.	I don't like the Bridge card game.	1.	Quite long, Ok catch you later.
B.	I guess I have made this letter	2.	Friendliest creatures in the sea.
C.	Dolphins are regarded as the	3.	Kingdom, the more I am astonished.
D.	The more I learn about the animal	4.	It is simply one of the most selfish games.

Codes

	A	B	C	D		A	B	C	D
(a)	1	4	3	1	(b)	4	1	2	3
(c)	3	1	4	2	(d)	2	3	1	4

47. State True of False for the following statements, T stands for True and F stands for False.

1. The robbers robbed every one of their belongings in the state transport bus.
2. There is a test today therefore it seems that the teacher has forgotten about it.

(a) 1-T, 2-F
(b) 1-F, 2-T
(c) 1-F, 2-F
(d) 1-T, 2-T

48. Consider the following statements.

A. Scientists have suggested that have a language on their own.

B. They usually produce sonar waves which can travel long distances.

C. They also suggest that whales are the largest mammals.

Which of the following statements are grammatically correct?
(a) B and C (b) A and C
(c) A and B (d) All of these

49. Match the following.

List-I	List-II	List-II
A. Matthew worked hard	1. Her course as she had	I. Lifted by little Chetan.
B. She must complete	2. Dance classes under	II. University attending fees.
C. The wooden chairs	3. To pay for his foreign	III. Her Guru's guidance.
D. She had been attending	4. Were too heavy to be	IV. Paid a good amount.

Codes

(a) A-4-1, B-3-IV, C-2-II, D-1-III
(b) A-4-1, B-1-IV, C-2-II, D-3-II
(c) A-3-1I, B-1-IV, C-4-I, D-2-III
(d) A-2-I1, B-1-III, C-4-II, D-3-III

50. Find the mismatched pair from the sentences containing idioms and their meanings given in brackets.

(a) I was hoping for 10K for the compensation but received only 6.5K, anyways half a loaf is better than none-(getting less than what one wants is better than not getting anything).

(b) Jumping from the moving train or similar stunts that children perform to imitate movie heroes in real life is like playing with fire-(if you do something dangerous or adventurous without full prepartion, you may get harmed).

(c) You are planning to quit your job at this point of time, I would say look before you leap (consider all consequences before taking an action).

(d) I sold my old laptop for small amount but I am sure the buyer will sell it at high price after refurbishing it, one man's junk is another man's treasure. (sometimes you get so focused on small details that you may miss the larger context).

PRACTICE SET 

1 Mark Questions

Directions (Q. Nos. 1-5) Read the passage carefully and select the option that you consider the most appropriate answer to each question.

Dolphins are regarded as the friendliest creatures in the sea and stories of them helping drowning sailors have been common since Roman Times.

The more we learn about dolphins, the more we realize that their society is more complex than people previously imagined. They look after other dolphins when they are ill, care for pregnant mothers and protect the weakest in the community, as we do.

Some scientists have suggested that dolphins have a language but it is much more probable that they communicate with each other without needing words. Could any of these mammals be more intelligent than man?

Certainly, the most common argument in favour of man's superiority over them that we can kill them more easily than they can kill us is the least satisfactory. On the contrary, the more we discover about these remarkable creatures, the less we appear superior when we destroy them.

1. From the passage, we come to know that dolphins
   (a) don't want to be with us as much as we want to be with them.
   (b) are proven to be less intelligent than once thought.
   (c) have a reputation of being friendly to humans.
   (d) are the most powerful creatures that live in the oceans.

2. What does the expression '… the fact that we can kill dolphins more easily than they can kill us …' mean? Or what does the writer want to convey through this?

(a) The dolphins are better adapted to their environment than we are.
(b) The dolphins have a very sophisticated form of communication.
(c) It proves that dolphins are not the most intelligent species at sea.
(d) It does not mean that we are superior to them.

3. One can infer from reading of the passage that
   (a) Dolphins are quite abundant in some areas of the world.
   (b) Communication is the most fascinating aspect of the dolphins.
   (c) Dolphins have skills that no other living creatures have such as the ability to think.
   (d) Dolphins have some social traits that are similar to those of humans.

4. What is the opposite meaning word of 'Remarkable'?
   (a) Striking   (b) Worthy of attention
   (c) Common place   (d) Ordinary

5. The expression 'least satisfactory' means
   (a) Unsatisfactory
   (b) Lowest level of satisfaction
   (c) Most significant
   (d) Unacceptable

Directions (Q. Nos. 6 and 7) Fill in the blanks using correct tense of the verb given in the brackets immediately after the blank and accordingly select the best option.

6. Men .... (*not manage*) to abolish wars up to now but maybe they will find a way in the future.
   (a) never managed
   (b) did not manage

(c) have never managed

(d) will have never managed

7. Robinson Crusoe .... (*puzzle*) when he .... (*discover*) the print of a foot on the sand.

(a) was puzzled, discovered

(b) is being puzzled, had discovered

(c) puzzled, discovered

(d) puzzling, is being discovered

8. Fill in the correct form of tenses.

Computers can be .... by the mischief makers using ....

(a) Damage, false information

(b) Damaged, computer virus

(c) Spoiled, computer program

(d) Shut down, keybord

Directions (Q. No. 9 and 10) Find the antonym of the word underlined in the sentence by choosing the correct option.

9. The government is taking measures to augment the country's food supply.

(a) prohibit

(b) decrease

(c) surpass

(d) compensate

10. Jatin Thakur is a very well-known painter of the contemporary art.

(a) Creative   (b) Modern

(c) Newest   (d) Very old

Directions (Q. No. 11 and 12) Choose the synonym of the underlined words in the sentences given below.

11. Your explanation that your social commitments tie you down, does not convince me.

(a) parties   (b) welfares

(c) restrictions   (d) obligations

12. He used to regale us with anecdotes.

(a) Bore   (b) Flatter

(c) Entertain   (d) Explain

Direction (Q. No. 13) Change the following sentence into passive voice so that it expresses the same idea and accordingly choose the correct option.

13. The people regarded him as an imposter and called him a villain.

(a) He would be regarded by the people as an imposter and called a villain.

(b) He is regarded as an imposter by the public and called a villain.

(c) He was regarded as an imposter and called a villain by the people.

(d) He has been regarded as an imposter by all and called a villain.

14. Change the sentence into active voice.

The committee's recommendation was voted by the presiding officer.

(a) The presiding officer voted for the committee's recommenation.

(b) The recommendation vote was given by the presiding officer.

(c) The presiding officer gave the vote for the committee's recommendation.

(d) The vote for recommendation was with the presiding officer.

Direction (Q. No. 15) Change the sentence into direct speech. Choose the correct option.

15. Jack asked his mother to cheer up because he would go and get work somewhere.

(a) Cheer up," mother,. I'll go and get work somewhere'', said Jack.

(b) "Cheer up mother, I'll go and get work somewhere, "? said Jack.

(c) "Cheer up mother," said Jack "I'll go and got work somewhere"

(d) "Cheer up, mother, I'll go and get work somewhere'', said Jack.

16. Change the sentence into indirect speech.

My mother said to me, " (no space) May you succeed in your examinations."

(a) My mother asked me to succeed in the upcoming examinations.

(b) My mother wished to me that I may succeed in the examinations.

(c) My mother wished me that I might succeed in the examinations.

(d) My mother expressed me that I might be succeeding in the examinations.

Directions (Q. Nos. 17 and 18) Fill in the blanks with suitable determiners or articles. Select the correct option from the given choices.

17. What…nice mother she is. She takes care of…small need of her children.
(a) the, each
(b) the, all
(c) a, each
(d) a, every

18. My friend is … sailor. After finishing his education, he took up … job with the Merchant Navy. … job is extremely interesting. It takes him all over … world.
(a) a, the, An, a
(b) a, an, The, the
(c) a, the, The, a
(d) a, a, The, the

Direction (Q. No. 19) Fill in the blanks with the most suitable conjunction and select the option accordingly.

19. English is … difficult to speak … difficult to write and understand.
(a) neither…nor
(b) not only…but also
(c) though, yet
(d) either…or

20. Fill in the blank with suitable conjunction.
……. the test was very difficult, all the students got one hundred per cent in it.
(a) So
(b) Although
(c) For
(d) As

Direction (Q. No. 21) Select the option nearest to the meaning of the idiom underlined in the given sentence.

21. He <u>took to heart</u> the death of his wife as he was very much attached to her.
(a) was shocked by
(b) was ruined by
(c) was deeply affected by
(d) was condoled by

22. Find the meaning of the given proverb. Still waters run deep
(a) Don't make trouble; do what others are doings
(b) Be quiet; shut your mouth
(c) In a place you are not comfortable
(d) A quiet or placid manner may conceal a passionate nature.

23. Fill in the blank with the suitable phrasal verb.
Abhi spent a long time looking for houses but eventually …….. the one near his office.
(a) decided upon
(b) bought
(c) decided onto
(d) went to

Direction (Q. No. 24) Punctuate the given sentence to make it meaningful and accordingly choose the best option.

24. none of tellyrands sayings is more famous than this speech was given to man to conceal his thoughts
(a) None of tellyrands sayings is more famous than this; 'speech was given to man to conceal his thoughts.'
(b) None of tellyrands sayings is more famous than this; speech was given to man to conceal his thoughts.
(c) none of Tellyrands' sayings is more famous than this; ''Speech was given to man to conceal his thoughts''.
(d) None of Tellyrand's sayings is more famous than this: "Speech was given to man to conceal his thoughts".

Directions (Q. Nos. 25 and 26) Fill in the blanks with the most appropriate verb form and choose the correct option accordingly.

25. I think, we ……. go out for shopping today because we need a lot of things for the picnic. We ……. make sure that we carry a first aid box too. We ……. even need some ropes in case we decide to go trekking.
(a) must, must, should
(b) should, may, may
(c) should, must, may
(d) should, might, may

26. She ……. sleep in the verandah. We have a spare room for her.
(a) dare not
(b) should not
(c) need not
(d) might

Directions (Q. Nos. 27 and 28 Fill in the blanks with appropriate prepositions. Choose from the options.

27. At the eleventh hour he withdrew .... the contest, leaving the field open .... his opponent.
(a) of, from
(b) from, of
(c) from, to
(d) for, to

28. A child is not able to distinguish good .... evil. Death does not distinguish .... the rich and the poor. Sir Ronald Ross is distinguished .... his medical researches.
(a) by, for, between
(b) from, between, for
(c) from, among, for
(d) from, between, of

Directions (Q. Nos. 29 and 30) Find the option which is different from the others in any respect from the four options given.

29. (a) Flare
(b) Glint
(c) Shimmer
(d) Simmer

30. (a) Nun
(b) Monk
(c) Knight
(d) Priest

Directions (Q. Nos. 31 and 32) In the passages below, the first and last sentences are identified as A and Z. The remaining four sentences are labelled as P, Q, R and S. Find the correct sequence of these four sentences and select the correct option.

31. A : The earliest reference to the playing card has been found in China, as long ago as the tenth century.
P : They appeared in Italy around 1320.
Q : Long before that the Chinese used paper money which was similar in design to the playing cards.
R : It is believed that perhaps travelling gypsies introduced them to Europe.
S : In olden days cards were used both for telling fortune and playing games.

Z : The current pack of 52 cards was only regulated in the seventeenth century.

The options are
(a) QSRP
(b) SQPR
(c) RQSP
(d) PQRS

32. A : Fireworks have become a common thing nowadays; in fact, special events are now incomplete without bursting them.
P : The impact it has on the environment and the health of the people is worrisome.
Q : Moreover, the bangs and fizzes it creates are loved by people.
R : Everyone loves the spectacular visions and colours in the sky.
S : However, all this show in only stunning to look at.
Z : We need to take measures to control the use of fireworks.

The options are
(a) SPQR
(b) RPSQ
(c) PRQS
(d) RQSP

33. At an interview if you are asked the question, "What is your educational background?", then the best response will be ---
(a) I studied how to build a software in college.
(b) I studied in a good English medium school and a famous college.
(c) I studied for a degree course in college.
(d) I studied Computer Engineering in my college.

34. To begin a small talk, which is the best option?
(a) You look great, what do you eat to remain healthy?
(b) Do you play any musical instrument, I play guitar?
(c) I am from Ranchi, where are you from?
(d) What are you doing this weekend?

Directions (Q. Nos. 35-40) An Article is given below with some parts missing but substituted by blanks with numbers 35-40. Identify the text by which the numbers may be substituted from the options given below.

Benefits of Travelling

by Mushir Ranjan

Travelling is man's instinctive behaviour. Man has been travelling since time immemorial to satisfy

....**(35)**...., to ....**(36)**.... new lands, to search for food and for pleasure. Travelling gives us ....**(37)**.... to disconnect from our regular life. We get to forget our problems or issues for a few weeks. It can also help us ....**(38)**.... which we would not have understood without travelling. Travelling is like a ....**(39)**.... that has a lot more to give than most people are willing to accept. When travelling with friends or relatives, ...**(40)**.... which will create a lifelong bond that nothing can erase. So, travelling has got numerous benefits and one should always be willing to fly to newer avenues to remove stress and to acquire and learn more by travelling to newer areas.

35. (a) his inquisitiveness
    (b) his imagination
    (c) his want
    (d) either (a) or (b)

36. (a) explore   (b) search
    (c) acquire information
    (d) be well informed

37. (a) a moment   (b) an excuse
    (c) an opportunity   (d) an encounter

38. (a) to figure things out
    (b) to reason
    (c) to find out
    (d) to explore

39. (a) good stress remover
    (b) best stress buster
    (c) best change
    (d) best opportunity

40. (a) memories stored for a life time
    (b) creates memories for ever
    (c) long lasting memories
    (d) we will store memories

2 Marks Questions

41. Choose the correct option to fill in and complete the set of sentences.
    1. The teacher .... (write) on the green board with a marker.
    2. She .... (want) to explain the law of gravitation with the help of a diagram.
    (a) had been writing, had wanted
    (b) is writing, wants
    (c) has written, wanted
    (d) writes, want

42. Arrange the parts sequentially to make a meaningful sentence.
    A. of approximately 40 per cent of the
    B. the central
    C. part of South America drains an area
    D. the amazon basin that lies in
    E. continent with its perennial rivers
    (a) DBCAE   (b) ACBDE
    (c) BEADC   (d) DAEBC

43. Replace the underlined words with the correct words.

    A380 is the world's <u>more noisy</u> airplane, making half of the noise generated by its contemporary aircrafts. It is due to the state of the art engineering and latest technology that the aircraft <u>have been winning</u> the Noise Abatement Society award for its silent functioning.
    (a) Too noisy, had been winning
    (b) More noiseless, won
    (c) Most noisy, winning
    (d) Most noiseless, won

44. Find the pair of words that are different from the others.
    (a) Vibrant-lifeless   (b) Native- foreign
    (c) Attire- traditional
    (d) Cosmopolitan- rural

45. Replace the words in bold with the correct words.

Although the lack of **lithosphere**, water and for that matter the unavailability of any other usable resource indispensible for the humankind will be an **matter of fact** hindrance for such a painstakingly hi-tech mission, yet **crowd** are very much sanguine about the lunar tourism prospects.

(a) Atmosphere, mistakable foreigners
(b) Hydrosphere, obvious, world
(c) Biosphere, total, people
(d) Atmosphere, obvious, people

46. Match the following.

List-I	List-II
A. Quadrant Foxtrot is an area on	1. To look for usable resource on the moon.
B. NASA also has sent various missions	2. Its first hotel on the moon.
C. The Grand hotel is constructing	3. Land on the surface of the moon.
D. Apollo 11 is the first space craft to	4. The surface of the moon.

Codes

	A	B	C	D			A	B	C	D
(a)	1	4	3	1		(b)	4	1	2	3
(c)	3	1	4	2		(d)	2	3	1	4

47. State true of False for the following statements, T stands for True and F stands for False.

1. An ecosystem is where organism interact with one another and there environment.
2. A balanced ecosystem is indispensible for biotic and abiotic bacteria to thrive with effort.

(a) 1-T, 2-F   (b) 1-F, 2-T
(c) 1-F, 2-F   (d) 1-T, 2-T

48. Consider the following statements.
A. Place like offices, hospitals and universities had restricted the use of mobile phones.
B. The Traffic Police Department has also restricted its use while driving a motor vehicle.
C. Still a large number of people do not follow these restrictions.

Which of the following statement/s are grammatically correct?
(a) B and C
(b) A and C
(c) A and B
(d) All of these

49. Match the column A with column B to complete the sentences.

Column A		Column B
A. His trip	1.	was gifted to her.
B. The house	2.	was not fed properly.
C. The doll	3.	was sponsored by his company.
D. The camel	4.	was dressed up beautifully.

Codes
(a) A-3, B-1, C-4, D-2
(b) A-3, B-1, C-2, D-4
(c) A-1, B-3, C-4, D-2
(d) A-1, B-3, C-2, D-4

50. Find out the meaning of the underlined word.

His brother's worthy suggestions changed Sachin to a <u>steadfast</u> cricketer.
(i) determined   (ii) firm
(iii) famous   (iv) committed
(a) (i), (ii), (iii)
(b) (i), (ii), (iv)
(c) (i), (iii), (iv)
(d) (ii), (iii), (iv)

ANSWERS

Chapter 1   Noun

1. (b)	**2.** (a)	**3.** (d)	**4.** (b)	**5.** (a)	**6.** (d)	**7.** (a)	**8.** (b)	**9.** (c)	**10.** (d)
11. (b)	**12.** (a)	**13.** (b)	**14.** (a)	**15.** (a)	**16.** (c)	**17.** (b)	**18.** (d)	**19.** (c)	**20.** (b)
21. (d)	**22.** (d)	**23.** (b)	**24.** (d)	**25.** (a)	**26.** (c)	**27.** (c)	**28.** (c)	**29.** (c)	**30.** (a)
31. (a)	**32.** (b)	**33.** (b)	**34.** (d)						

Chapter 2   Pronoun

1. (b)	**2.** (a)	**3.** (a)	**4.** (c)	**5.** (d)	**6.** (a)	**7.** (d)	**8.** (c)	**9.** (a)	**10.** (d)
11. (b)	**12.** (a)	**13.** (d)	**14.** (b)	**15.** (b)	**16.** (a)	**17.** (d)	**18.** (c)	**19.** (d)	**20.** (d)
21. (a)	**22.** (b)	**23.** (d)	**24.** (a)	**25.** (b)	**26.** (b)	**27.** (c)	**28.** (c)	**29.** (b)	**30.** (c)
31. (b)	**32.** (c)								

Chapter 3   Verbs

1. (b)	**2.** (a)	**3.** (d)	**4.** (b)	**5.** (d)	**6.** (d)	**7.** (b)	**8.** (c)	**9.** (b)	**10.** (d)
11. (a)	**12.** (d)	**13.** (b)	**14.** (a)	**15.** (d)	**16.** (b)	**17.** (a)	**18.** (b)	**19.** (b)	**20.** (c)
21. (c)	**22.** (c)	**23.** (b)	**24.** (d)	**25.** (b)	**26.** (c)	**27.** (b)	**28.** (a)	**29.** (c)	**30.** (c)

Chapter 4   Adverbs

1. (b)	**2.** (c)	**3.** (a)	**4.** (d)	**5.** (b)	**6.** (c)	**7.** (c)	**8.** (c)	**9.** (c)	**10.** (b)
11. (c)	**12.** (a)	**13.** (c)	**14.** (b)	**15.** (b)	**16.** (c)	**17.** (b)	**18.** (c)	**19.** (d)	**20.** (a)
21. (a)	**22.** (d)	**23.** (c)	**24.** (b)	**25.** (d)	**26.** (b)	**27.** (c)	**28.** (c)	**29.** (b)	

Chapter 5   Adjectives

1. (d)	**2.** (d)	**3.** (b)	**4.** (b)	**5.** (d)	**6.** (a)	**7.** (b)	**8.** (c)	**9.** (a)	**10.** (c)
11. (a)	**12.** (d)	**13.** (d)	**14.** (c)	**15.** (b)	**16.** (b)	**17.** (c)	**18.** (c)	**19.** (b)	**20.** (b)
21. (b)	**22.** (a)	**23.** (a)	**24.** (d)	**25.** (c)	**26.** (b)	**27.** (a)	**28.** (c)	**29.** (b)	**30.** (c)
31. (b)	**32.** (c)	**33.** (c)	**34.** (c)	**35.** (b)	**36.** (c)				

Chapter 6   Articles

1. (c)	**2.** (d)	**3.** (b)	**4.** (b)	**5.** (a)	**6.** (a)	**7.** (a)	**8.** (b)	**9.** (a)	**10.** (a)
11. (b)	**12.** (b)	**13.** (c)	**14.** (b)	**15.** (a)	**16.** (c)	**17.** (d)	**18.** (d)	**19.** (a)	**20.** (c)
21. (a)	**22.** (d)	**23.** (d)	**24.** (c)	**25.** (b)	**26.** (c)	**27.** (b)	**28.** (i)(b) (ii)(b)	**29.** (b)	**30.** (a)
31. (c)	**32.** (d)	**33.** (b)	**34.** (c)	**35.** (a)					

Chapter 7   Prepositions

1. (a)	**2.** (c)	**3.** (c)	**4.** (a)	**5.** (d)	**6.** (c)	**7.** (a)	**8.** (c)	**9.** (b)	**10.** (c)
11. (b)	**12.** (b)	**13.** (b)	**14.** (b)	**15.** (a)	**16.** (b)	**17.** (a)	**18.** (c)	**19.** (b)	**20.** (b)
21. (b)	**22.** (d)	**23.** (a)	**24.** (a)	**25.** (d)	**26.** (b)	**27.** (a)	**28.** (a)	**29.** (c)	**30.** (b)
31. (a)	**32.** (c)	**33.** (a)	**34.** (d)	**35.** (b)	**36.** (d)				

Chapter 8   Conjunctions

1. (b)	2. (b)	3. (a)	4. (c)	5. (d)	6. (a)	7. (d)	8. (b)	9. (b)	10. (a)
11. (b)	12. (b)	13. (b)	14. (b)	15. (a)	16. (a)	17. (c)	18. (a)	19. (d)	20. (b)
21. (c)	22. (c)	23. (c)	24. (a)	25. (a)	26. (b)	27. (c)	28. (a)	29. (a)	30. (c)
31. (b)	32. (c)	33. (b)	34. (a)						

Chapter 9   Tenses

1. (a)	2. (c)	3. (c)	4. (c)	5. (d)	6. (b)	7. (b)	8. (a)	9. (d)	10. (a)
11. (b)	12. (b)	13. (d)	14. (a)	15. (b)	16. (b)	17. (b)	18. (b)	19. (b)	20. (a)
21. (b)	22. (a)	23. (a)	24. (a)	25. (c)	26. (b)	27. (b)	28. (c)	29. (b)	30. (d)
31. (d)	32. (b)	33. (c)	34. (b)						

Chapter 10   Active and Passive Voice

1. (c)	2. (a)	3. (c)	4. (b)	5. (d)	6. (b)	7. (a)	8. (b)	9. (c)	10. (b)
11. (c)	12. (a)	13. (a)	14. (a)	15. (c)	16. (b)	17. (a)	18. (d)	19. (a)	20. (a)
21. (a)	22. (a)	23. (a)	24. (a)	25. (a)	26. (b)	27. (b)	28. (a)	29. (a)	30. (c)
31. (c)	32. (b)								

Chapter 11   Direct and Indirect Speech

1. (b)	2. (c)	3. (c)	4. (a)	5. (a)	6. (c)	7. (b)	8. (b)	9. (a)	10. (c)
11. (a)	12. (b)	13. (c)	14. (b)	15. (b)	16. (c)	17. (b)	18. (c)	19. (b)	20. (a)
21. (a)	22. (b)	23. (c)	24. (a)	25. (c)	26. (d)	27. (a)	28. (b)	29. (a)	30. (b)
31. (b)	32. (d)								

Chapter 12   Error Detection

1. (b)	2. (a)	3. (c)	4. (d)	5. (a)	6. (a)	7. (c)	8. (b)	9. (a)	10. (b)
11. (b)	12. (a)	13. (c)	14. (b)	15. (c)	16. (b)	17. (a)	18. (c)	19. (d)	20. (c)

Chapter 13   Sentence Arrangement

1. (b)	2. (c)	3. (c)	4. (b)	5. (b)	6. (a)	7. (d)	8. (c)	9. (b)	10. (a)
11. (d)	12. (c)	13. (b)	14. (d)						

Chapter 14   Fillers

1. (b)	2. (a)	3. (d)	4. (b)	5. (c)	6. (c)	7. (d)	8. (d)	9. (c)	10. (a)
11. (c)	12. (a)	13. (c)	14. (b)	15. (b)	16. (d)	17. (a)	18. (b)	19. (c)	20. (b)

Chapter 15   Synonyms and Antonyms

1. (b)	2. (c)	3. (b)	4. (d)	5. (b)	6. (d)	7. (d)	8. (c)	9. (a)	10. (b)
11. (b)	12. (b)	13. (c)	14. (c)	15. (b)	16. (b)	17. (c)	18. (b)	19. (d)	20. (b)
21. (c)	22. (d)	23. (a)	24. (c)	25. (d)	26. (b)	27. (d)	28. (a)		

Chapter 16   One Word Substitution

1. (c)	2. (a)	3. (c)	4. (b)	5. (d)	6. (b)	7. (c)	8. (c)	9. (b)	10. (a)
11. (a)	12. (b)	13. (c)	14. (a)	15. (d)	16. (b)	17. (a)	18. (c)	19. (b)	20. (a)
21. (c)	22. (b)	23. (a)	24. (b)	25. (a)	26. (c)	27. (a)	28. (c)	29. (d)	

Chapter 17   Idioms and Phrases

1. (b)	2. (b)	3. (d)	4. (c)	5. (b)	6. (b)	7. (d)	8. (c)	9. (b)	10. (a)
11. (c)	12. (c)	13. (a)	14. (b)	15. (d)	16. (a)	17. (b)	18. (b)	19. (a)	20. (c)
21. (d)	22. (a)	23. (c)	24. (b)	25. (c)					

Chapter 18   Reading Comprehension

1. (c)	2. (a)	3. (c)	4. (d)	5. (d)	6. (b)	7. (b)	8. (d)	9. (c)	10. (d)
11. (b)	12. (c)	13. (d)	14. (b)	15. (b)	16. (c)	17. (d)	18. (c)	19. (b)	20. (c)

Chapter 19   Writing Skills

1. (a)	2. (b)	3. (d)	4. (b)	5. (b)	6. (c)	7. (a)	8. (c)	9. (c)	10. (a)
11. (b)	12. (b)	13. (c)	14. (b)	15. (a)	16. (c)	17. (d)	18. (b)	19. (c)	20. (c)
21. (d)	22. (d)	23. (b)	24. (a)	25. (c)	26. (b)	27. (a)	28. (a)	29. (c)	30. (c)
31. (d)	32. (c)								

Chapter 20   Communication Skills

1. (b)	2. (a)	3. (b)	4. (d)	5. (b)	6. (a)	7. (d)	8. (b)	9. (d)	10. (c)
11. (a)	12. (c)	13. (c)	14. (a)	15. (c)	16. (d)	17. (a)	18. (c)	19. (d)	20. (b)
21. (c)	22. (d)	23. (a)	24. (b)	25. (d)	26. (b)				

Practice Set 1

1. (c)	2. (d)	3. (c)	4. (b)	5. (b)	6. (b)	7. (b)	8. (b)	9. (d)	10. (d)
11. (c)	12. (c)	13. (a)	14. (b)	15. (b)	16. (c)	17. (a)	18. (c)	19. (c)	20. (d)
21. (b)	22. (b)	23. (c)	24. (c)	25. (b)	26. (c)	27. (a)	28. (c)	29. (c)	30. (b)
31. (b)	32. (a)	33. (a)	34. (d)	35. (c)	36. (c)	37. (a)	38. (c)	39. (b)	40. (a)
41. (c)	42. (b)	43. (c)	44. (c)	45. (c)	46. (b)	47. (a)	48. (a)	49. (c)	50. (d)

Practice Set 2

1. (c)	2. (d)	3. (d)	4. (d)	5. (b)	6. (c)	7. (a)	8. (b)	9. (b)	10. (d)
11. (d)	12. (c)	13. (c)	14. (a)	15. (d)	16. (c)	17. (d)	18. (d)	19. (b)	20. (b)
21. (c)	22. (d)	23. (a)	24. (d)	25. (c)	26. (c)	27. (c)	28. (b)	29. (d)	30. (c)
31. (a)	32. (d)	33. (d)	34. (c)	35. (a)	36. (a)	37. (c)	38. (a)	39. (a)	40. (d)
41. (b)	42. (a)	43. (d)	44. (c)	45. (d)	46. (b)	47. (b)	48. (a)	49. (a)	50. (b)